DEALING WITH
UNRESOLVED CONFLICT

FORGIVENESS
THROUGH THE LENS
OF HEAVEN

KEN MCFARLAND

Published by

Maurice Wylie Media

Your Inspirational & Christian Publisher

For more information visit
www.MauriceWylieMedia.com

Endorsements

Having a book written from one who can identify with the difficulties that affected many because of the 'Troubles', on the topic of forgiveness that has caused many to question their faith; how can I forgive if there is no repentance, is greatly welcomed. In this succinct book, Ken enables the reader to navigate the complexities of forgiveness from biblical foundation that is conditional upon repentance. Through his analysis, many will find affirmation, comfort, assurance, and hope, while equally encouraging and challenging the reader to reflect on how they live out those same truths in the present.

Rev. Canon Alan Irwin, BTH, CCS.
The Diocese of Clogher, County Fermanagh, Northern Ireland.

The subject of forgiveness is crucial in relationships, but also be complex and controversial. Ken McFarland brings us a study of it that is courageous, clear and careful; he stays close to Biblical text, references the contest in Northern Ireland, and demonstrates deep pastoral concern. Whatever your thoughts are on forgiveness, this reflection will enlighten, edify and help you examine your views again. It contains both comfort and challenge. It covers all aspects of the subject and made me want to trust God more fully, love my neighbour more faithfully who has sinned against me and aim for relationships that are fully healed and glorifying to God.

Rev. Dr. David Cupples BABD, (Retired minister).
Enniskillen Presbyterian Church, County Fermanagh, Northern Ireland.

Contents

Foreword

As a person of faith, I've carried the burden of this deeply emotional topic of forgiveness for over a decade, due to the murder of my husband, David Black. The weight of it has often felt overwhelming, compounded by the expectations of fellow Christians and the strong opinions expressed by society at large. Before delving into this book, I must admit that while I was curious, I also harboured some scepticism.

However, the author, drawing from a comprehensive foundation of evidence, adeptly navigates the intricate terrain of biblical forgiveness through the lens of God's teachings. He does so in a gentle and compassionate manner. This approach has genuinely provided me with a clearer perspective, as Ken challenges both past and present narratives.

I would like to express my gratitude for granting me the opportunity to read this book. It has been a genuine privilege. It has helped me find answers to the multitude of questions I've carried. In fact, I intend to read it again.

I wholeheartedly recommend and extend an invitation to all who share similar struggles or hold opinions on the concept of biblical forgiveness to read and contemplate this book.

On the whole, this journey has been profoundly enlightening for me, instilling a genuine sense of hope.

Yvonne Black

In loving memory of my husband, David Black, who lost his life to the New IRA on November 1, 2012.

Preface

There are few Christian doctrines as challenging as forgiveness, not least because the issue of forgiveness lies at the very heart of the Gospel message itself, as evidenced in Jesus' own words, *"My blood…is poured out for many for the forgiveness of sins"* (Matthew 26:28 ESV). And yet sadly, so few understand what Jesus Himself actually taught about forgiveness and the vital role it plays, not only in the believer's relationship to God, but also in the believers' relationships with those around us.

In Christian bookstores today we find a great many books which seek to address the difficult subject of forgiveness. Some of these works will contain accounts of wrongs having been committed against an individual, whereupon the injured party embarks on a journey which ultimately leads to, what I will term for now, a "forgiving experience," after which it is claimed that God then grants a release from all those negative thoughts of hatred, bitterness, and even revenge. Such works, which often contain heart-rending accounts of wrongdoing, are primarily designed to appeal to the emotions, and as a consequence, even though they purport to present a Biblical example of forgiveness, there is little in-depth examination of the relevant Biblical texts on the subject.

While other authors will seek to present a biblically based examination of forgiveness, the "modern trend" I will contend, is almost always towards the downplaying of repentance, and the promotion of "unconditional forgiveness." The outworking of this approach places all the emphases on the Christian believer to forgive in every circumstance, regardless of the offence committed against them, and whether or not the offender has displayed any sign of remorse, let alone having genuinely sought forgiveness. Such an approach enables the respective authors to avoid the awkward scenario whereby an unremorseful offender, or an unpalatable biblical doctrine might thwart a happy ending. Nonetheless, the uncomfortable fact remains, that in the real world, a world tainted by sin, happy endings are not always possible.

The purpose of this book, therefore, is to examine true Biblical forgiveness in the light of such a real-world scenario, namely that of post-conflict Northern Ireland. A conflict which in its latest phase, lasted officially from 1969 to 1998, and cost over 3,500 lives. Often romantically portrayed as a struggle between "Irish freedom fighters" and an "occupying British Army," the hard facts reveal a very different story in that 80% of the fatalities were native-born Irish citizens either from Northern or Southern Ireland, while only 13.8% of those murdered were regular British Army personnel who had been drafted into Northern Ireland after the conflict started, to help the local police force maintain law and order.[1]

Moreover, with 90% of all murders during the conflict having been committed by paramilitary terrorist organisations (approximately 60% attributed to the Irish Republican Army and 30% attributable to pro-Union loyalist paramilitary groupings), and with a murder clearance rate of under 50%,[2] the implications regarding a lack of closure for many bereaved relatives are only too obvious. It is further the case that the deep-seated sectarian animosities which motivated the killings, coupled with the personal nature in which numerous victims were targeted, serve only to make the subject of forgiveness extremely difficult to broach.

Writing in 2001, Irish historian Tony Stewart summarises the consequences of the recent conflict when he states: *"A new set of bitter memories has been added to that of the 1920s, which is still raw, so that the population is more polarised than at any time in the last century."*[3] Regarding this study of forgiveness as intended, therefore, it is my sincere prayer that God is glorified as the only authoritative source of wisdom in this fallen world, and that through the 'truth' of the Bible, many will be called to consider the messages of Jesus, the one who *"loved righteousness and hated lawlessness"* (Hebrews 1:9).

---

[1]Liam Kennedy, *Who Was Responsible For The Troubles* (McGill – Queens University Press, 2020), 67.
[2]Joint Authors (William Matchett) *The Northern Ireland Question, Perspectives on Nationalism and Unionism* (Wordsworth Publishing 2020), 209.
[3]A.T.Q. Stewart, The Shape of Irish History (The Blackstaff Press Limited, Belfast, 2001), 181.

Introduction

Since the end of the Northern Ireland conflict in 1998, much has been written on the subject of reconciliation between the two opposing communities, namely those in favour of maintaining the constitutional link with the United Kingdom (Unionists), and those in favour of establishing a political United Ireland (Irish Nationalists/Republicans). As a welcome move away from the men of violence spilling "blood," political commentators, church representatives and many other well-meaning interested parties, have in turn spilt much "ink," in the noble quest of achieving a framework for lasting peace, free from the threat of politically motivated violence.

Much of the discussion in the early stages of this peace process revolved around the view that to prevent a return to violence, the causes, or in some respects even the perceived causes of the conflict, had to be addressed. As such, under the terms of the 1998 Belfast Agreement (also called the Good Friday Agreement) the Provisional Irish Republican Army (PIRA) and their political wing Sinn Fein, accepted the "principle of consent," which stated that the constitutional position of Northern Ireland could only be altered with the consent of a majority vote of the population in favour. On that basis, it was agreed that a new Northern Ireland devolved administration be established. This new administration was to take the form of a mandatory coalition assembly in which representatives of all political parties (including those affiliated with terrorist organisations) had a seat in Government as of right, albeit with their numerical representation in the new assembly based on their respective electoral mandate. Other measures included the early release of terrorist prisoners, the reforming and rebranding of the police force, the standing down of all other military personnel and the subsequent closure of many military and police installations.

A Fragile Peace

Broadly speaking, it is true to say that as these measures were implemented, a fragile peace took hold, although it was also the case that a sizeable minority from both sides of the political divide remained sceptical. While the leading protagonists, in the form of the Provisional IRA and Sinn Fein, supported the initiative, others from within Irish republicanism were opposed to the peace process, primarily because their ultimate goal of a "United Ireland," had not been achieved. As a consequence, therefore, terrorist splinter groups (IRA dissidents) were to emerge from that quarter, with the result that, albeit at a much-reduced level, there is still a credible threat of violence emanating from within this latest brand of violent Irish republicanism.

Many from the Unionist community were also extremely reticent as regards some of the concessions on offer to the terrorist organisations, not least the early release of terrorist prisoners, which was viewed as a travesty of justice. However, a majority of the Unionist community, desirous for some kind of peace and stability, did in time come to support the proposals and subsequently voted for the Belfast Agreement which facilitated the formation of the mandatory power-sharing coalition government in 1998. While it is not disputed that Northern Ireland as a whole, is a much better place today, the long-term stability which many craved, has in many respects remained elusive, in that the devolved assembly has undergone long periods of suspension due to fractious disagreements among the elected representatives.

A Gaping Wound

Having set the scene as to where Northern Ireland is today (2023), there remains one *gaping wound* which to date has not been addressed. I refer to the anguish and sense of injustice felt by the many victims and survivors of paramilitary terrorism, on both sides of the political/religious divide. While for them, the early release of convicted terrorists was a particularly difficult pill to swallow, they were to be given some comfort with the assurance that criminal cases emanating from the conflict would remain open, and where evidence was available to convict the perpetrators, they would still have to answer for their crimes.

However, with the passage of time, this process has produced very little by way of results. One reason for the lack of convictions emanates from the fact that a wealth of forensic evidence was lost when, as part of the decommissioning process, the terrorist organisations were permitted to destroy their own weaponry in circumstances which ruled out any examination of the firearms in question. As a consequence, victims and survivors feel betrayed, marginalised and ignored, concluding rightly or wrongly, that for the sake of maintaining the peace process, the pursuit of justice for their murdered relatives, and for those who still carry the scars of the conflict, has been relegated to the bottom of the priority list. Justice denied therefore, has served only to compound the pain.

Salt in the Wound

In such a scenario, particularly within the broadly Christian conservative culture of Northern Ireland, it is not surprising that church leaders would seek to contribute with a view to bringing some degree of comfort and reconciliation to bear. Unfortunately, however, this well-meaning contribution has often served only to pour salt into the aforementioned "gaping wound" in that the modern trend among theologians is to promote unconditional forgiveness i.e., the view that the injured party must forgive the offender even if that same offender remains unremorseful. Consequently, the marginalisation of victims and survivors in the political arena is often replicated in the ecclesiastical realm, as the views expressed by religious leaders simply do not resonate with the ongoing experience of those living with the consequences of the wrongs inflicted upon them.

In the context of today's Northern Ireland, it is also the case that the anguish of victims and survivors is further compounded in that the promotion of this unconditional forgiveness is taking place against a backdrop in which unrepentant terrorists and their political representatives, continue to reinterpret the historical narrative with a view to justify past atrocities and eulogize those responsible.

The Pain Alleviated

It is my intention therefore within this study to go some way to alleviating much of the anguish which many victims and survivors continue to experience today. Again, it is my proposition that a correct understanding of Biblical forgiveness, may in time allow many to see the Northern Ireland conflict through the lens of a Christian worldview. Having established such a framework, it would be my desire that a recognition of the truth that there is still a sovereign God in control of world events, will enable many to find that solace in the face of adversity, which has hitherto proved elusive.

Acknowledging, however, that the solutions to those problems which have beset us for centuries, are to be found in the Revealed Word of an all-knowing God, does not come without its challenges. Oftentimes when forgiveness and reconciliation are discussed from a Christian perspective, Jesus' teaching to, *"love your enemies"* and *"pray for those who spitefully use you and persecute you"* are rightly highlighted. Sadly however, in the context of the raw emotions associated with the Northern Ireland conflict, such divine instruction seems impossible to many, with the result that there becomes a "disconnect" between those who are hurting on the one hand, and the only source who can bring that much-needed comfort, on the other. Seeking to bridge this disconnect, and in so doing, open the way to comfort, hope, and even perhaps closure, is, therefore, the ultimate goal of this book.

Chapter One

Omagh 1998

Saturday, August 15 1998, was a glorious sunny day in the Tyrone market town. Shoppers were out in force, their numbers bolstered by parents and children in search of school uniforms for the soon-coming new academic term. My shift as a police officer with the Royal Ulster Constabulary was due to finish early, and I was looking forward to making the most of the good weather later. That was until the phone call. "A car bomb has been left at the town Courthouse," said the caller. Within ten minutes, High Street and the area around the Courthouse were cleared of pedestrians. "If anything goes off now, at least no one will be injured," I said to myself. Suddenly, about 300 hundred metres away, just out of sight in Market Street, there was a thunderous explosion…. The caller had given the wrong location for the bomb. As I ran towards the scene of the blast, people were running in the opposite direction. I tried to ask them if anyone is injured, but it's as if I am invisible. With a look of terror in their eyes, they just keep on running. Then I saw the toppled pushchair…. Surely, there can't have been children involved?

***

The death toll, which would eventually reach twenty-nine, comprising men, women, and children, plus two unborn infants, would represent the heaviest loss of life in any single terrorist attack in the history of the Northern Ireland Troubles. In the immediate aftermath, I felt a strong calling to anchor my thoughts and emotions in the God whom I had ignored for the majority if not all my life. Having not attended a church for over twenty years, however, I was to rely initially on prayer and reading extracts from the Bible, but alas, I didn't seem to be getting many answers.

Four months had passed when one Sunday morning at work, I had gone to take a break in the restroom. Sitting alone, I notice a discarded newspaper close by. Absentmindedly picking it up, my attention was drawn to the cover story, which was about a young girl called Sandy, who had been seriously injured in the Omagh bombing, and following a slow and painful journey, was now on the road to recovery. Sandy also recounted how on the day of the atrocity she had been standing beside her 21-year-old friend Julia, who had been killed instantly when the bomb had exploded only a matter of feet away.

As I continued to read the article, I was completely unaware that the story would prove much more significant than I could ever have imagined. Within Sandy's account of the bombing and the immediate aftermath, she made reference to a police officer who had taken a few minutes to hold her hand and offer some words of comfort. Regretting that she had never found out who he was, she said she would like him to know how much it meant, and to say thank you. Suddenly, the penny dropped, and looking again at Sandy's photo, the memories came flooding back, including the sights, sounds and smells of that traumatic day, as I realised that I was the police officer to whom Sandy referred.

Gathering my thoughts, I began to consider for the first time that perhaps some good had come out of that terrible atrocity after all. However, by way of testifying to her Christian faith, Sandy was to witness to the fact that such a scenario, although remote as far as I was concerned, was very much a biblical concept. Quoting a passage which had given her so much encouragement during those difficult times, Sandy referred to Romans 8:28, which reads: *"And we know that all things work together for good to those who love God, to those who are the called according to His purpose."*

Although a common passage for many Christians, as a fledgling believer at that time, this truth was relatively new to me. However, as I pondered these words, I began to take comfort in the fact that throughout all that had happened, there remained a sovereign God in control and that ultimately, He would work out His plan for good. In time, I had the pleasure of meeting Sandy who very graciously thanked me again in person for taking the time to offer a few words of comfort on that fateful day. However, I was at pains to add, that in the providence of God, I had so very much more to be thanking her for instead.

As the years have progressed, the Sovereignty of God revealed in Romans 8:28 has become the bedrock of my faith, and as I would go on to discover, this truth also plays a significant role when it comes to addressing forgiveness and reconciliation, particularly when conflicts remain unresolved. True confidence in a God whom we believe to be both sovereign and good, enables us to trust Him even amid those difficult circumstances we all must face from time to time.

Spurred on by the knowledge that nothing happens by accident and by implication seeking to make sense, not only of the extraordinary circumstances I had found myself in but also seeking to discover what wider plan God might be working out in a society riven by division, I developed a keen interest in the study of God's word. My journey also took me through several doctrinally diverse worship environments, including a period of full-time theological study before I settled into my current church community in 2014.

As I look back now on those years of searching, there was one experience which stands out amongst all others, and which I now believe was pointing me in the direction of this present study. It was while reading the story of the patriarch Joseph, and in particular the account of his eventual reconciliation with his estranged brothers. The picture of Joseph weeping uncontrollably as he is overcome by love for his siblings, despite the awful way they had treated him in the past, gave me hope for the future as I pondered such an embrace taking place in our divided society.

Like the story of Joseph, however, the path to forgiveness and reconciliation can be a difficult journey for those involved. Seeking a resolution based on our terms, and relying solely on our own understanding, will inevitably be doomed to failure. Turning rather to a sovereign God who is working out His plan for humanity, and recognising His divine wisdom as regards true forgiveness and reconciliation I will contend, provides us with the only sustainable pathway to lasting peace.

Chapter Two

Enniskillen 1987

On the afternoon of Sunday, November 8, as Mrs Joan Wilson and her husband Gordon made their way home from Enniskillen hospital, the outside world was little more than a blur of passing sounds and colours; and yet their inner world had been turned upside down and would never be the same again. Just a few hours earlier, Mrs Wilson had been playing the church organ in the local Methodist church where she attended every Sunday morning. Unexpectedly however on this occasion, events were to take a traumatic turn, when Mrs Wilson noticed a man in military uniform enter the church. After a brief word with someone at the rear of the sanctuary, the man whom Mrs Wilson now realised was someone she knew well, hurriedly made his way up the isle and proceeded directly towards her. It was only then that she was to learn of the terrible events which were unfolding at the town cenotaph.

Earlier that morning, Mrs Wilson's husband Gordon, along with their 20-year-old daughter Marie, had gone to the local War Memorial in Enniskillen, to pay their respects at the annual Remembrance Day service. Just as the service was about to get underway, an IRA bomb, which had been strategically concealed close to the cenotaph, exploded, killing eleven people and injuring countless others. (A twelfth victim, Mr Ronnie Hill, was to die from his injuries, following several years in a coma).

Gordon Wilson was among the many people who had been injured as a result of the explosion and was subsequently conveyed to Enniskillen Hospital, and it was here that Mrs Wilson was reunited with her husband. The relief of finding her husband alive and displaying relatively minor injuries, however, was to be short-lived. As concern grew for their daughter's condition, the couple would eventually learn that Marie had succumbed to the injuries she had sustained and had passed away. As they travelled back to their Enniskillen home, the couple attempted to gather their thoughts and tried to come to terms with the events of the previous few hours. As they did so, Mrs Wilson recounts how her husband was to become acutely aware of two things they would need to sustain them in the days ahead, namely, great *strength* and *wisdom*.

During a television interview recorded the day after the atrocity, Gordon Wilson, having recounted the last words he had exchanged with his daughter as she lay under the rubble of the collapsed building where the bomb had been concealed, went on to say how he bore no ill will towards the perpetrators. Holding back the tears for his daughter, Gordon further revealed that the night after the bombing, he had prayed for the men responsible, asking God to forgive them.

In the ensuing clamour for a headline, the world's media misrepresented Mr Wilson's petition to God and declared that Gordon Wilson had actually forgiven the men responsible for his daughter's murder. In many quarters today, this false representation continues, particularly among those who would seek to promote unconditional forgiveness. Pastor Russ Parker, for example, describes Gordon Wilson's words as an "act of forgiveness,"[4] when in fact the reality was something very different.

Pondering again Gordon Wilson's remarkable witness during those hastily arranged media interviews in the days after the atrocity, one can only conclude that in his time of need, God did indeed equip Gordon with both great strength and wisdom. Although missed by many, I will propose that Gordon Wilson epitomised the very essence

---

[4]Russ Parker, *Forgiveness is Healing* (Society for Promoting Christian Knowledge, London, 2011), 29.

of the Christian teaching on forgiveness, and in so doing fulfilled to the letter, our Lord's command in Matthew 5:44 to show love to our enemies, to do good towards those who hate you, and pray for those who persecute you. However, it must also be stressed that at no time did Gordon Wilson actually forgive those responsible for the murder of his daughter and the other innocents who died on that fateful day.

Gordon Wilson would go on to clarify exactly what he meant when he appeared on a prime-time television programme sometime later. In stating again that he bore no ill will, or held no grudge against those responsible for the bombing, and that he would continue to pray for the perpetrators, the following point was put to Mr Wilson by the chat show host, Terry Wogan: "You also said that you couldn't forgive, because forgiveness was not within your power." Again displaying remarkable wisdom, Gordon replied, "**Only God can forgive**, [and most importantly Gordon added] **and on His** [God's] **terms**."[5]

Here, I will argue, is the essence of Christian forgiveness. And yet many theologians continue to promote a different forgiveness, a forgiveness with *no terms* at all. A forgiveness which I will contend, has only served to discredit Biblical teaching in the eyes of many who have suffered as a consequence of the actions of wicked unremorseful men. Seeing no substance nor indeed justice in the proposition that forgiveness is to be given in all and every circumstance, I say again, has created a disconnect between those who seek to bring comfort and hope from a Christian perspective, and those who are in so much need of that same comfort and hope today.

I reiterate again that it will be my desire throughout the remainder of this book, to seek to bridge that disconnect by way of a simple straightforward exegesis of the relevant texts which, when taken together, reveal the Divine plan for true forgiveness and reconciliation.

---

[5]https://www.youtube.com/watch?v=6C-aBS3TvCM – Accessed 16/02/2022

Chapter Three

Love Covers a Multitude of Sins

I have the pleasure of conducting a weekly Bible class for young teenagers as part of our church programme. As such, the challenge is always to keep things simple, without diluting or diminishing the gospel message. While it goes without saying that the Bible itself is central, next to that, I rely on commentaries and the writings of respected Christian theologians to gain further insight, and to maintain a level of interest among the students. That said, however, when it comes to many of our modern-day theologians, it is becoming increasingly necessary to first strip away some of the extra-Biblical concepts often brought to bear on the respective subjects under consideration.

This imposition of such concepts I will contend, is no less prevalent when it comes to the subject of biblical forgiveness. Consequently, the waters around the subject have become so muddied that it becomes almost impossible for the common man to be able to decipher truth from error. This muddying of the waters in relation to the subject of forgiveness I would suggest, is sadly evident among many respected Christian writers today.

For example, R.T. Kendall, in seeking to promote a new and hitherto unknown type of forgiveness which he terms "*total forgiveness,*" in his 2010 book of that name, makes the revealing claim that he had never, "been confronted by this message of total forgiveness by all of my heroes – both living and dead. I have read hundreds of sermons by the Puritans and Reformers yet I cannot recall being told by them that I must totally forgive or otherwise grieve the Holy Spirit."[6] In light of this revelation, it's tempting to suggest that perhaps there is a reason why Mr Kendall has not come across this particular type of "total forgiveness" among the many great theologians of the past, primarily because these theologians relied on Scripture alone for their edification, and as such, shunned the machinations of men.

Nonetheless, in proceeding to answer the question, "What is total forgiveness?" R.T. Kendall cites the view that at the crucifixion, "no one seemed very sorry at the cross of Jesus," and then quotes our Lord's response, *"Father forgive them, for they do not know what they are doing"* (Luke 23:34). By way therefore of laying the foundation for what is in effect unconditional forgiveness, Kendall then asserts, "By asking the Father to forgive them it showed *he* had forgiven them; he released all of them from their guilt." Kendall then concludes that this example of unconditional forgiveness in the face of wrongdoing, "must be our response as well."[7]

At first glance, it might seem that R.T. Kendal's conclusions, based on the passage quoted, are perfectly feasible and align with biblical teaching on the subject of forgiveness. However, as will be revealed, there is indeed a very good reason why Mr Kendall's so-called *new revelation* is not found in the "hundreds of sermons by the Puritans and Reformers" to which he refers.

Sadly, however, R.T. Kendall is not alone among modern-day writers who appear to have imposed extra Biblical concepts on scripture, in an attempt to interpret Biblical forgiveness. Another well respected theologian, whom I'm almost reluctant to mention, is the late Timothy Keller, not least because of the strong stand he had adopted against many of the liberalising tendencies within the Christian Church today. However, writing in what was to prove one of his last publications in 2022, titled; "Forgive, Why Should I And How Can I?" Timothy Keller I would also suggest, unwittingly adds to the confusion around the subject, as he too seeks to present unconditional forgiveness. The

---

[6]R.T. Kendall, *Total Forgiveness* (Hodder & Stoughton Ltd., London, 2001), 7.
[7]Ibid., 12-13

mixed picture which Timothy Keller paints is no better highlighted when within the closing pages of his book, he makes the following statements; first, he declares, "As we know, *you must repent* in order to be saved." This statement is followed on the next page with, *"Be kind and compassionate to one another, **forgiving each other, just as in Christ God forgave you"*** Ephesians 4:32. So far so good one might conclude, however just a few paragraphs later, in asserting that the believer is to be "endlessly forgiving," Timothy Keller adds, that in perusing the goal of a reconciled relationship, "God requires forgiveness whether or not the offender has repented and has asked for forgiveness"[8] (Mark 11:25). At face value, there is somewhat of a contradiction here. If God requires repentance in order to forgive sin, and the believer is to forgive as God forgives, how do we then arrive at the view that believers, are to forgive an offender even though there is no repentance let alone any desire on the part of the offender to seek forgiveness?

The answer to the dilemma, according to Timothy Keller, is found in examining the distinction between the forgiveness spoken of in Mark 11:25 which reads: *"And whenever you stand praying, if you have anything against anyone, forgive him,"* and the apparent contradiction contained in Luke 17:3 which states: *"If your brother sins against you, rebuke him; and if he repents, forgive him."* Although accepting himself that the former passage (Mark 11:25) when taken alone supports what Keller calls "cheap grace," and while also accepting that there are times when an offender should be "rebuked" (Luke 17:3),[9] Timothy Keller attempts to square the circle by proposing that "forgiveness can have two meanings." Keller elaborates; "Sometimes the forgiveness of which the New Testament speaks presupposes repentance on the part of the offender and sometimes not. Luke 17:3-4 is an example of the first, while Mark 11:25 is an example of the latter." In an attempt to clarify further, Timothy Keller adds:

> "...the word forgiveness is being used in two somewhat different ways. In Mark 11 "forgive them" means inwardly

---

[8]Timothy Keller, *Forgive Why Should I And How Can I?* (Hodder & Stoughton Ltd., London, 2022), 212-213.
[9]Ibid., 104-105.

being willing to not avenge oneself. In Luke 17 "forgive them"
means "reconcile to them". There is then, *a kind of forgiveness
that ends up being inward only and another kind that issues
outwardly* toward a possible restored relationship."[10]

In short, Keller goes on to propose that this "inner" forgiveness "must
always happen" and is therefore *unconditional,* while "outward"
forgiveness only applies when "the perpetrator recognises his wrongdoing
and repents or does not."[11] At face value there appears little wrong with
Keller's interpretation here, however, it must be pointed out that when
we rely on Scripture alone, we read nothing about different "aspects,"
or "kinds" of forgiveness. Rather, as will be explained throughout this
study, forgiveness as regards the believer, is presented as an act which is
fulfilled either by, covering an offence in love (which is the case in Mark
11:25) or, for those more serious offences, granting forgiveness when
the correct circumstances are met (Luke 17:3).

While it is true that even the smallest transgression is still regarded
as sin (James 2:10), it is nonetheless true that there are degrees of sin
(Luke 12:47-48). Bearing this principle in mind, it is the nature of
the offence, therefore, which determines the course of action adopted
by the offended party when granting forgiveness. That said however,
it should be stressed that in the case of those more serious offences,
the prevailing stance *within* the offended party must be, with the
help of God's grace, to seek to nurture an attitude of a *willingness to
forgive* - again, if and when the appropriate circumstances are met.
Consequently, in distinction from the view espoused by Keller, who
presents both "inner forgiveness" (before any remorse or repentance
on the part of the offender) and "outward forgiveness" (following
repentance) as an act of Biblical forgiveness, it must be noted that
as regards Biblical forgiveness, there is a very real difference between
actually forgiving someone and being *willing to forgive.*

By way of seeking further support for his particular interpretation
of Biblical forgiveness, Timothy Keller appeals to the parable of the

[10]Ibid., 106
[11]Ibid., 107

"unforgiving servant" (Matthew 18:21-35), the primary lesson of which he asserts is the fact that the King had mercy on the debtor and released him from his debt. Keller concludes therefore, "To cancel the debt (verse 27) brings us to the very heart of forgiveness. When the king forgave the debt, it means he absorbed the loss himself." While Timothy Keller rightly cautions against holding onto bitterness, he rather naively in my view suggests that as, "bit by bit by bit, you grant forgiveness in this way, eventually you'll begin to feel forgiveness."[12]

In light of this drift towards unconditional forgiveness therefore, it is not surprising that in his interpretation of the parable in question, Timothy Keller makes no mention of the repentance and pleas for mercy on the part of the original debtor before he was pardoned (verse 26). Rather, Keller's somewhat confusing take on the parable is further highlighted when he suggests that the original debtor's miss-treatment of *his* servant was, "Because the [first] servant does not respond to the king's forgiveness with genuine repentance and a changed life."[13] Such a scenario again appears to contradict biblical teaching in that nowhere is God (represented here by the King) ever seen to grant forgiveness *before* there has been repentance on the part of the sinner. While I am fully aware that some would seek to challenge this last statement concerning the nature of God's forgiveness, let me assure the reader that all the relevant texts on forgiveness will be examined in due course, whereupon they can decide for themselves the necessity or otherwise of repentance before forgiveness can be granted.

In attempting therefore to avoid the accusation of muddying the waters myself however, let us return to the passage from 1 Peter 4:8 which formed the basis for the title of this chapter; *"Above all, keep loving one another earnestly, since love covers a multitude of sins."* The first point I would make is that this is not God's love in view here, simply because God's love ultimately covers *all* believers' sins. Rather, the love here in 1 Peter 4, is that love expressed by the Christian as they forgive a multitude of sins which are committed against them, or which they witness taking place, time and time again throughout everyday life.

---

[12]Ibid., 9.
[13] Ibid., 9.

Consequently, within this context, it is vitally important to note that the passage implies that *love does not cover all sins*. By way of substantiating this view, we see that Jesus himself alludes to the fact that some sins are more serious than others when in Matthew 18:15 and Luke 17:3, He teaches that there are indeed times when a matter cannot simply be overlooked. Sadly however, as we will see, the very thought that those more serious offences might prove to be occasions where forgiveness itself should be withheld until repentance is forthcoming from an offender, has in effect become an alien concept to many theologians today, and it is to challenge this mindset that I humbly present the following study.

Chapter Four

We Never Walk Alone

It is often said of the Ulster-Scots people that while they may be industrious and hardworking, they also tend to be stubborn, or to put it in their own dialect, *thran*. In such an environment, seeking to change long-established ideas and customs, particularly by subterfuge or stealth, will be met with fierce resistance. This principle is no more evident than among those who have remained faithful to their Christian roots, and who remain firm in what is termed, "The Reformed Faith."

While this trait, I will argue, is for the most part commendable, the hard-heartedness which sometimes accompanies such a mindset, is one of those negative characteristics which is warned against in the pages of Scripture, and, as we will learn, is of particular significance in relation to the subject of forgiveness. Bearing in mind again, the context and the background within which I have chosen to place this study, it would be naïve in the extreme to ignore the real possibility that the influences of community and culture, will to some extent, have an influence on the subject at large.

Theologian and author, David Augsburger, highlights the significance of this issue in his book, "The New Freedom of Forgiveness" when he writes:

> "Community surrounds us, shapes our lives, and guides our formation of values.... It shapes our most basic understandings.... even our understanding of the Bible.

No one reads the Bible alone. An invisible community of commentators and interpreters sits with each of us each time we open it. Each of us understands and interprets its teaching from a particular moment in the centuries and from a particular culture and context; we seek to build a bridge of understanding between the biblical world of two thousand years to our present situation."[14]

Sober reflection on this truth again reveals that all are vulnerable to outside influences and must always be on guard against such. Indeed, as I have already alluded, such influences, by way of man's sensibilities, are already shaping the present-day teaching around biblical forgiveness. The only bulwark I believe we have at our disposal is the unchangeable nature, and the grace of Jesus, as evidenced by the writer to the Hebrews when he declares; *"Jesus Christ is the same yesterday, today, and forever. Do not be carried about with various and strange doctrines. For it is good that the heart be established by grace"* (Hebrews 13:8-9).

As we look predominantly to the teaching of Jesus himself, therefore, and in simultaneously seeking His grace at every turn, we pray that those outside influences which would seek to negatively influence His teaching would be kept far away. To this end, let us proceed to look at the teaching of forgiveness, namely forgiveness as intended by the Divine Author.

Keeping Things Simple

It is often said that the plain things of Scripture are the main things of Scripture, and when another's theory contradicts that plain teaching, it is time to return to the spiritual edification and insight of the Scriptures themselves. With this statement in mind, it will be my intention to show that this truth is no less prevalent when it comes to the subject of biblical forgiveness, where sadly so many other theories abound today.

---

[14]David Augsburger, *The New Freedom of Forgiveness* ((Moody Publications, Chicago, IL. 2000), 79.

In appealing therefore to the plain teaching of Scripture as found within the Bible, and particularly within the teaching of Jesus Himself, my aim is to address forgiveness or what I have termed "forgiveness as intended," i.e. the forgiveness as intended by God, which when enacted, actually leads to reconciliation. This effectual forgiveness, therefore, I will show, stands in stark contradiction to what many liberal theologians and Christian leaders erroneously promote today as forgiveness - namely the view that one must forgive an offender unconditionally and, in all circumstances, regardless as to whether such an offender has expressed any remorse, or indeed any desire at all to be reconciled.

This liberal view which tellingly downplays the need for repentance, even in cases where the offence is so serious that Scripture itself demands the offender be confronted, is becoming all too common today. By way of evidence, I reference again Christian author R.T Kendall, who presents such a view in the introduction to his previously mentioned book titled, "Total Forgiveness." Kendal declares, "One must totally forgive those who will not be reconciled."[15] Author and Counsellor, June Hunt, also presents a similar view in her book, "Forgiveness the Freedom to Let Go." In promoting unconditional forgiveness, Hunt states that "To forgive means…. To release your right to hear "I'm sorry""[16]. June Hunt further declares, "forgiveness is an ongoing process which requires that you choose to forgive every time the offence comes to mind."[17]

During my research, I interviewed many victims and survivors to ascertain their respective views on forgiveness. Listening to these accounts, it became clear that there was one recurring theme which placed the Northern Ireland conflict apart from many other conflicts around the world. While the unconventional nature of the paramilitary violence perpetrated from behind the cover of the civilian population was unique in and of itself, it was the personal nature of the conflict as evidenced by how murder victims were targeted, particularly within

---

[15]R.T. Kendall, *Total Forgiveness* (Hodder & Stoughton Ltd, London, 2010), 10.
[16]June Hunt, *Forgiveness The Freedom To Let Go* (Hendrickson Publishers, Massachusetts, USA, 2013), 16.
[17]Ibid., 37.

those mixed rural communities which bordered the Irish Republic.

As regards violence perpetrated by Irish republicans, quite often it would be an only son of a farming family, singled out with a view to cutting off any lines of inheritance, thus causing entire families to move out of the area. In like manner, prominent business families and their businesses would be targeted, either by way of murdering family members or bombing their premises, again with the same objective of causing them to move away. As for Loyalist paramilitaries who operated predominantly in the urban environments, while these groupings claimed to be targeting known republicans, often innocent civilians were attacked simply because of their perceived religion, or the area they came from.

By way of further compounding the anguish of bereaved relatives following the murder of a loved one, it was not uncommon for members of grieving families to find themselves being taunted by those in support of the perpetrators, either by way of an anonymous phone call or even on occasion, in the public street. As can be imagined, such incidents leave lasting scars which are difficult, if not impossible to heal.

The failure of many religious leaders to properly address forgiveness within this climate, and in particular those who would promote unconditional forgiveness, coupled with the teaching that failure to forgive is itself a sin, do a grave injustice not only to bereaved relatives, but more importantly, to the Word of God, which when properly examined has the very real potential to bring healing even in those most difficult of situations. For June Hunt therefore, to suggest that "forgiveness is an ongoing process which requires that you choose to forgive every time the offence comes to mind," is akin to telling a rape victim to keep on forgiving their attacker, even though at every possible opportunity, he continues to smirk and sneer at her. This grotesque, not to mention unbiblical scenario, becomes even more untenable since Hunt also declares, "Not forgiving your offender is an offence to God, thereby making you an offender to God as well."[18]

---

[18]Ibid., 26.

The trend to overcomplicate biblical teaching, which has been alluded
to already, only serves further to sever the link between theologians,
teachers, and preachers on one side, and the common man or woman
on the other. As a consequence, many are put off studying the Bible
properly today, although it must be recognised that Bible study per
se has sadly declined amongst the laity in general. With this in mind,
it is my intention to appeal primarily to a straightforward exegesis
of all the relevant texts, safe in the knowledge that this basic Bible
study approach is sufficient to reveal the true nature of forgiveness as
intended by God.

Chapter Five

God's Forgiveness

Quoting Ephesians 4:32: *"be kind to one another, tenderhearted, forgiving one another, just as God in Christ forgave you"*, and Colossians 3:13; *"forgiving each other; as the Lord has forgiven you, so you also must forgive"* (ESV), Christian counsellor and author, Ken Sande, writes, "God has given us an incredibly high standard to live up to when we have the opportunity to forgive someone."[19] Forgiveness, therefore, is certainly not to be taken lightly, and as will be explored later, it often seems impossible to forgive someone in your own strength, especially when you have been the victim of a grievous wrong.

By way of teasing out what forgiveness itself actually entails, Ken Sande again initially lays out what forgiveness is *not*. First, forgiveness he contends, "is not a feeling. It is an act of will. Forgiveness [Sande continues] involves a series of decisions, the first of which is to call on God to change our hearts. As He gives us grace, we must then decide (with our will) not to think or talk about what someone has done to hurt us. God calls us to make these decisions regardless of our feelings."[20]

Secondly, forgiveness "is not forgetting." Forgetting, Sande elaborates, "is a *passive* process in which a matter fades from memory merely with the passing of time. Forgiving [on the other hand] is an *active* process; it involves a conscious choice and a deliberate course of action. To put it another way, when God says that He *"remembers your sins no*

---

[19]Ken Sande, *The Peace Maker A Biblical Guide to Resolving Personal Conflict*, (Baker Books, Grand Rapids, MI, 2004), 205.
[20]Idid., 206.

more" (Isaiah 43:25), He is not saying that He cannot remember our sins. Rather He is promising that He *will not* remember them. When [God] forgives us, He chooses not to mention, recount, or think about our sins ever again."[21] Finally Sande writes:

> "Forgiveness is not excusing. Excusing says, "That's okay," and implies, "What you did wasn't really wrong," or "You couldn't help it." Forgiveness is the opposite of excusing. The very fact that forgiveness is needed and granted, indicates that what someone did was wrong and inexcusable. Forgiveness says, "We both know that what you did was wrong and without excuse. But since God has forgiven me, I forgive you." Because forgiveness deals honestly with sin, it brings a freedom that no amount of excusing could ever hope to provide."[22]

Looking now to what forgiveness as God intended should entail, and appealing to the original Greek meaning and usage of the two respective words translated in the English Bible as "forgive," Sande again writes:

> *"Aphiemi,* a Greek word that is often translated as "forgive," means to let go, release, or remit. It often refers to debts that have been paid or cancelled in full (e.g. Matthew 6:12; 18:27, 32). *Charizomai,* another word for "forgive," means to bestow favour freely or unconditionally. This word shows that forgiveness is undeserved and cannot be earned (Luke 7:42-43; 2 Corinthians 2:7-10; Ephesians 4:32; Colossians 3:13)."[23]

David Augsburger also alludes to the respective connotations associated with the two Greek words in question when he writes, "The two Greek words for forgiveness are translated most clearly as "to release

---

[21]Ibid., 206.
[22]Ibid., 206.
[23]Ibid., 207.

or set free" and "to offer a gift of grace." Augsburger elaborates, "In the scriptural context, the meaning is always relational; it is addressing the actual interactions between offended people."[24] On the basis of these two definitions therefore from the original language it is clear that forgiveness can be enacted in two ways, either the debt which is incurred is paid or legally cancelled, or, as I will contend later, in the case of those more trivial sins, forgiveness is simply given as a gracious gift through love.

There are times therefore when forgiveness can be costly, in that when someone sins, they create a debt which must be paid. Most of that debt, as Ken Sande points out, "is owed to God" who in his great mercy "sent his Son to pay that debt on the cross for all who would trust in Him (Isaiah 53:4-6; 1 Peter 2:24-25; Colossians 1:19-20)."[25] However, if the sin has also been against someone, part of that debt is due to them, and as such they have a decision to make. Either they take payment on the debt by way of repentance and or reparation, or again, in the case of those many smaller "debts," one might choose to write off the debt in love, with a view to maintaining a reconciled relationship.

Where, however, a larger debt remains unpaid, the temptation is always to try and exact payments from an offender by way of, dwelling on past events associated with the wrong, inflicting emotional pain by way of slandering an offender, or lashing out in revenge. While these actions, as Ken Sande points out, "may provide a perverse pleasure for the moment," they will ultimately "exact a high price from you in the long run." Sande therefore issues this warning to anyone caught up in a spirit of bitterness towards an offender: "Unforgiveness is a poison we drink, hoping others will die."[26]

By way of taking a final look for now at what forgiveness entails, I refer to the Christian writer and pastor, Chris Brauns. In his book titled "Unpacking Forgiveness," he also cites the two passages quoted at the start of this chapter, Ephesians 4:32 & Colossians 3:13, and

---

[24]David Augsburger, *The New Freedom of Forgiveness* (Moody Publications, Chicago, IL. 2000), 29.
[25]Ken Sande, *The Peace Maker A Biblical Guide to Resolving Personal Conflict*, 207.
[26]Ibid., 208.

declares that when it comes to defining forgiveness, we must start with the principle that, "God expects believers to forgive others in the way He forgave them." Elaborating on this basic truth therefore, Brauns summarises, "God's forgiveness for Christians is the model He expects Christians to live out."[27]

In seeking to explore further how God forgives, Brauns first makes mention of the truth that we all need God's forgiveness, "because everyone has offended God."[28] The Apostle Paul declares in Romans 3:10: *"There is none righteous, no, not one."* And a few verses later, in Romans 3:23, Paul states again, *"all have sinned and fall short of the glory of God."* A correct understanding of biblical forgiveness, therefore, coupled with a willing disposition towards honesty and humility, will show that the need for forgiveness is the great leveller. Most of us, however, continues Brauns, "tend to compare ourselves to other people. Comparing by that standard, we may not seem so bad. But we are not accountable to measure up to other people. We answer to a perfectly holy and just God."[29]

Second, Brauns points out that, "While God's forgiveness is gracious, it is not free." In reiterating the reformed doctrine that the sinner is saved "only by grace"[30] (Ephesians 2:8-9), Brauns reminds us that the debt that we owed was paid by our Saviour Jesus Christ on the cross of Calvary. Forgiveness, therefore, is not free, because Christ had to pay the penalty to satisfy the perfect justice of God.

Third, Pastor Brauns also reminds us that, "God's forgiveness is conditional. Only those who repent and believe are saved".[31] Repentance requires a turning away from our own understanding, a turning away from sin; while faith requires a turning *to* Jesus Christ and trusting in Him alone for our understanding. Repentance and faith therefore go hand in hand, just as the apostle Paul declares in Acts 20:20-21: "I kept back nothing that was helpful, but proclaimed

---

[27]Chris Brauns, *Unpacking Forgiveness* (Crossway, Wheaton, Illinois, 2008), 44.
[28]Ibid., 45.
[29]Ibid., 45.
[30]Ibid., 46.
[31]Ibid., 47.

it to you, and taught you publicly and from house to house, testifying to Jews, and also to Greeks, repentance toward God and faith toward our Lord Jesus Christ."

Fourth, "God's forgiveness is a commitment," a commitment Brauns declares is the "essence of God's forgiveness" in that when the sinner is justified and declared righteous, there is a commitment given that our sins will never be held against us again.[32]

Fifth, God's forgiveness "begins the process of reconciliation." This is one of the main distinctions between false unconditional forgiveness, particularly that forgiveness which someone might "grant" to an unrepentant offender, in the belief that granting such will be rewarded with some therapeutic benefit for the one who has been wronged, as opposed to true biblical forgiveness which, according to Brauns, is "inextricably linked to reconciliation," and in effect, "No one is forgiven by God without being reconciled to God."[33] This basic truth is presented by the Apostle Paul in 2 Corinthians 5:17-21:

> *"Therefore, if anyone is in Christ, he is a new creation; old things have passed away; behold, all things have become new. Now all things are of God, who has reconciled us to Himself through Jesus Christ, and has given us the ministry of reconciliation, that is, that God was in Christ reconciling the world to Himself, not imputing their trespasses to them, and has committed to us the word of reconciliation. Now then, we are ambassadors for Christ, as though God were pleading through us: we implore you on Christ's behalf, be reconciled to God. For He made Him who knew no sin to be sin for us, that we might become the righteousness of God in Him."*

Sixth, "God's forgiveness does not mean the elimination of all consequences." Though it is true that, *"There is therefore now no condemnation to those who are in Christ Jesus, who do not walk according to the flesh, but according to the Spirit,"* it is also true that, "This side of

---

[32]Ibid., 47.
[33]Ibid., 48.

heaven, we [believers] will continue to work through the consequences of our rebellion against God."[34] While the truth that a loving God from time to time finds it necessary to discipline his wayward children will be examined in detail later, suffice to say at this juncture, "God disciplines his children so they will understand the seriousness of sin and will increasingly conform to the image of his son."[35]

Finally, with all of these aspects of God's forgiveness in mind, Chris Brauns, rightly in my view, defines true forgiveness as:

> A commitment by the one true God to pardon graciously those who repent and believe so they are reconciled to Him, although this commitment does not eliminate all consequences.[36]

In proclaiming the Bible as our sole authority as regards this issue, I concur with Chris Brauns again when he declares, "I write with the firm conviction that only God's Word can unpack forgiveness. [God] has spoken clearly and sufficiently through his word. God has given us all that we need for life and godliness through our knowledge of him who called us by his own glory and goodness (2 Peter 1:3)."[37]

---

[34] Ibid., 49.
[35] Ibid., 51
[36] Chris Brauns, *Unpacking Forgiveness* (Crossway, Wheaton, Illinois, 2008), 51.
[37] Ibid., 15.

Chapter Six

What Saith the Scriptures?

In turning to the scriptures, I remind the reader that those passages which present biblical forgiveness, deal with relationships in *two* distinct areas. First of all, we have the "vertical" relationship, which is concerned with God's relationship to the believer specifically, and to humanity in general; and secondly, we have the "horizontal" relationship, which encompasses the believer's relationship with fellow believers, and everyone else within the wider community in which they live. While these two different relationships are unique in and of themselves, there are nonetheless, consistent principles which pertain to forgiveness which transcend both, and which we can apply to many of the conflicts and disagreements we face in our everyday lives.

In 1 John 1:8-9 for example, a core principle of forgiveness is plainly set forth as follows: "If we say that we have no sin, we deceive ourselves, and the truth is not in us. If we confess our sins, He is faithful and just to forgive us our sins and to cleanse us from all unrighteousness." Commenting on this passage, Chris Brauns states:

> God does *not* forgive all. God's forgiveness is conditional. It should be conditional in our relationships too. For sure, we must have an attitude of grace or willingness to forgive all people. We are commanded to love our enemies and to pray for those who persecute us (Mathew 5:43-48). But complete forgiveness can only take place when there is repentance.[38]

---

[38]Chris Brauns, *Unpacking Forgiveness* (Crossway, Wheaton, Illinois, 2008), 21.

R.T. Kendall on the other hand, as highlighted earlier, takes a very different view. Citing Jesus' statement on the cross, *"Father forgive them, for they do not know what they do"* (Luke 23:34), he states, "If He [Jesus] had waited until they felt any guilt or shame for their words and actions, then Jesus would never have forgiven them."[39]

On the contrary, I will show that a correct understanding of Jesus' prayer request on the cross does not negate the primary role of repentance in the process of effectual forgiveness. Proceeding to examine the role which forgiveness plays in God's dealing with fallen humanity, it is appropriate at this stage to address those misconceptions which arise from a superficial interpretation of Jesus' statement as recorded in Luke 23:34, and indeed several other pronouncements by Jesus which are often cited to downplay the role of repentance, if not negating the need for repentance altogether.

Father Forgive Them

First off, even though Jesus undoubtedly has the power to forgive sin, as witnessed in the accounts of the healing of the paralytic man (Luke 5:20-24) and the story of the sinful woman (Luke 7:49), it is clear that Jesus did not actually forgive any of those who participated in or condoned his crucifixion. And neither was it the case that Jesus was simply asking God to let the offenders off. Christian author, Jay Adams, also points out: "If, indeed, Jesus unconditionally forgave those who crucified Him, then, of course, that would mean that they had been forgiven without hearing or believing the Gospel." Clearly that teaching is heretical Adams concludes.[40] Rather, the truth of the matter is simply that Jesus prayed that those responsible would be forgiven in the course of time. In keeping with the biblical criteria for forgiveness therefore, Jesus was in effect praying that God would bring those responsible to a recognition of their sin, and in so doing, to a position of repentance and faith.

---

[39] R.T. Kendall, *Total Forgiveness* (Hodder & Stoughton Ltd, London, 2010), 33.
[40] Jay E. Adams, *From Forgiven to Forgiving* (Calvary Press, Amityville, NY, 1994), 28.

Indeed, there is every merit in the view that the repentant thief who was one of two criminals crucified alongside Jesus on that terrible day, and who only a short time earlier had mocked Jesus along with others (Matthew 27:44), embodied the first of many converts in answer to the Messiah's prayer. Having been brought to a recognition of his own fallen nature before the sinless Messiah (Luke 23:41), and by implication having displayed repentance and faith, the thief was able to declare, *"Lord, remember me when You come into Your kingdom"* (Verse 42). Jesus subsequently pronounces this man's innocence and declares, *"Assuredly, I say to you, today you will be with Me in Paradise"* (Verse 43).

Further evidence which points to an almost spontaneous answer to Jesus' petition is also found in the statement made by a Roman Centurion present at the crucifixion. As a military officer commanding one hundred men, this Centurion was most probably the officer in charge of events surrounding the crucifixion, and as such would have commanded the soldiers responsible for scourging Jesus before dressing him in a mock robe and putting a crown of thorns on his head (Matthew 27:27-30; Luke 22:63-64). Ultimately, this same Centurion would have overseen the nailing of Jesus to the cross.

As events unfolded however, under an eerie darkness which had supernaturally engulfed the scene, and as an earthquake heralded the death of the Messiah, the Roman Centurion was heard to declare, *"Truly this Man was the Son of God!"* (Mark 15:39). Matthew's account presents a little more detail and reads, *"the centurion and those with him, who were guarding Jesus, saw the earthquake and the things that had happened, they feared greatly, saying, "Truly this was the Son of God!"* (Matthew 27:54).

In Luke's account we have perhaps a little prelude to the ultimate response to Jesus' petition, "Father forgive them" when we read, *"And the whole crowd who came together to that sight, seeing what had been done, beat their breasts and returned"* (Luke 23:48). Pastor and theologian John MacArthur comments on this closing scene:

> "Hours before, this had been a bloodthirsty mob, shrieking with vicious delight for the death of Jesus. Now that they had what they wanted, it left them with nothing more than despair, grief, and horror. The triumph they expected left them hollow and hopeless. The crowd dispersed, and everyone slunk back into their homes in fear. The beating of the breasts signified alarm and a measure of remorse."[41]

With the Holy Spirit already beginning to work in the hearts of the people to bring them to a position of repentance, we see the climax of the Spirit's calling on the Day of Pentecost just fifty days later. The apostle Peter, when speaking to the assembled crowd, many of which would appear to have been present at the crucifixion, declared to them, *"Therefore let all the house of Israel know assuredly that God has made this Jesus, **whom you crucified,** both Lord and Christ"* (Acts 2:36). Continuing in the next verse, we see the effect this statement had on the people: *"Now when they heard this, they were **cut to the heart,** and said to Peter and the rest of the apostles, "Men and brethren, what shall we do?"* To which Peter replied, *"**Repent,** and let every one of you be baptized in the name of Jesus Christ for the remission of sins; and you shall receive the gift of the Holy Spirit"* (Acts 2:37-38).

Finally, we witness the culmination of God's response to Jesus' petition from the cross when, *"those who gladly received his word were baptized; and that day about **three thousand souls** were added to them"* (Acts 2:41). Author and Bible teacher, Arthur Pink comments on the power of our Lord's dying petition:

> "We are shown here the efficacy of prayer. This Cross-intercession of Christ for His enemies met with a marked and definite answer. The answer is seen in the conversion of the three thousand souls on the Day of Pentecost. I base this conclusion on Acts 3:17 where the apostle Peter says, "And now, brethren, I wot that through ignorance

---

[41] John F. MacArthur, *The Freedom and Power of Forgiveness* (Crossway Books, Wheaton, Illinois, USA, 1999), 50.

ye did it, as did also your rulers." It is to be noted that Peter uses the word "ignorance" which corresponds with our Lord's "they know not what they do." Here then is the Divine explanation of the three thousand converted under a single sermon. It was not Peter's eloquence which was the cause but the Saviour's prayer."[42]

The Stoning of Stephen

On a similar theme, it has also been stated that the apostle Stephen, regarded as the first Christian martyr, unconditionally forgave those who stoned him to death. The account is recorded in Acts 7:59-60, where we read, *"And they stoned Stephen as he was calling on God and saying, "Lord Jesus, receive my spirit." Then he knelt down and cried out with a loud voice, "Lord, do not charge them with this sin." And when he had said this, he fell asleep."* Referencing this passage, Timothy Keller, in seeking to justify his view of unconditional forgiveness writes, "When Stephen died praying, *"Lord, do not hold this sin against them,"* it is clear that there was no repentance from the wrongdoers, since they were stoning and killing him as he spoke. *Yet Stephen forgave them."*[43]

Pastor Chris Brauns, however, correctly points out that "Stephen's prayer for those who stoned him closely parallels the interceding prayer of Jesus on behalf of his tormentors.... But again, it could be pointed out that Stephen did not say to those stoning him, "I forgive you."[44] Rather, like Jesus, Stephen prayed that in the fullness of time, those responsible would be brought to a position where their sins would be wiped away, leaving no 'charge' to face." Nonetheless, Stephen's plea for mercy on the part of his assailants, even though he did not actually forgive them, displays a right attitude of the heart in that, Stephen displayed a genuine desire that those who were stoning him would be brought to a position of repentance and faith and thus forgiven of their crime.

---

[42]Arthur W. Pink, *The Seven Sayings of the Saviour on the Cross* (Parker Books, Brand Rapids, MI, 2005), 21
[43]Timothy Keller, *Forgive Why Should I And How Can I?*, 106.
[44]Chris Brauns, Unpacking Forgiveness, 145-146.

Again, the biblical account bears witness to an answer to Stephen's dying prayer in that the apostle Paul (formerly Saul), one of the most zealous persecutors of the early Christians, and who had actually supervised the stoning of Stephen (Acts 7:58), was miraculously converted not long after while journeying to Damascus (Acts 9:1-20). The subsequent contribution which the apostle Paul was to make to the early Christian Church, bears perfect testimony to the truth that great good can often come out of even the most wicked deeds (Romans 8:28).

The Paralytic Man and Sinful Woman

Despite the assertions of some proponents of unconditional forgiveness like theologian Steve Chalke, who boldly proclaims that Jesus went about "forgiving people on the hillsides, in their own houses and out in the streets",[45] the truth of Scripture rather declares that there are only two instances recorded where Jesus did pronounce forgiveness upon individuals. Both accounts appear in Luke's gospel, namely, the healing of the paralytic man who was lowered down through the roof by four of his friends into a house where Jesus was ministering (Luke 5:18-25), and the account of the sinful women who anointed Jesus feet with precious oil (Luke 7:37-50). Both accounts require a little examination, not least because those who promote the view that repentance is not a requirement for forgiveness, cite both these incidents as evidence for their stance. For example, Pastor and author Russ Parker, in seeking to promote the view that there was no repentance on the part of either recipient prior to Jesus forgiving their sin, states: "What is even more remarkable is that in the two specific cases mentioned of Jesus forgiving individuals, there is not one word spoken by the person in need."[46]

The problem with adopting such a position is that the primary lesson taught within both these accounts is downplayed, if not

---

[45]Steve Chalke, *The Lost Message of Jesus* (Zondervan, Grand Rapids, Michigan, 2003), 105.
[46]Russ Parker, *Forgiveness is Healing* (Society for Promoting Christian Knowledge, London, 2011), 9.

missed altogether. Indeed, it could be said that Russ Parker's writing embodies just such a scenario and misses the point entirely. In seeking to disparage those who hold the view that repentance is a necessary prerequisite to forgiveness, he states: "It was the generous and liberal way in which Jesus forgave that so incensed and aroused the opposition of some scribes and Pharisees."[47] On the contrary, as is highlighted in both of these accounts where first the paralytic man, and later the sinful woman are declared forgiven by Jesus, the objection raised by the scribes and Pharisees centred solely on the deity of Christ.

This is evidenced in the reactions of the scribes and Pharisees as recorded first of all in Luke 5:21 when, after Jesus had declared to the paralytic man, "your sins are forgiven you" (v 20), we read that, *"the scribes and the Pharisees began to reason, saying, "Who is this who speaks blasphemies? Who can forgive sins but God alone?"* And again in Luke 7:49, we see this similar reaction among the Pharisees after Jesus had declared the sinful woman forgiven when we read: *"And those who sat at the table with Him began to say to themselves, "Who is this who even forgives sins?"*

Having determined therefore that it was the visible display of Jesus' deity in the presence of his main detractors, which was the focal point of both accounts, let us conclude this aspect of our study by addressing the view that our Lord may also have intended to reveal some new teaching on repentance and forgiveness in these passages. First of all, it must be stressed that the view that Jesus bestowed forgiveness on either the paralytic man or the sinful woman without a word of repentance, is an argument from silence, and by implication constitutes weak exegesis; not to mention the fact that such a stance would contradict Jesus' clear instruction as recorded by Luke just a few chapters later, where our Lord Jesus declares on two occasions, *"unless you repent you will likewise perish"* (Luke 13:3 & 5).

Secondly, by virtue of the fact that in both accounts, Jesus was able to see into the hearts and minds of those who were opposed to His teaching

---

[47]Ibid., 2.

(Luke 5:22; Luke 7:39-40), is it not also perfectly feasible to assume that Jesus could also see into the hearts of those whom he would go on to pronounce forgiven? And indeed, again in both accounts, we see that Jesus did make specific reference to the faith of both the paralytic man (Luke 5:20) and the sinful woman (Luke 7:50).

Returning for a moment however to the scene where the paralytic man is lowered through the roof, and reading verse 20 again, "When He [Jesus] saw their faith, He said to him, *"Man, your sins are forgiven you."* Some detractors would seek to point out that the term "their faith" refers only to the four friends who lowered the paralytic man down, and not the paralytic himself. In reply, it is fairly obvious that the entire party are in view here, and again, without labouring the point, Jesus' actions would not have contradicted His own clear teaching in Luke 13:3, 5. Clearly therefore, had the faith of either the paralytic man or the sinful woman, been less than genuine, and *not* born out of heartfelt repentance, then Jesus would have compromised His own standards when he declared them to be forgiven.

In relation to the account of the sinful woman, as found in Luke 7:36-49, Matthew Henry writes in his Bible commentary:

> "It is true this woman has been a sinner: he [Jesus] knows it; but she is a pardoned sinner, which supposes her to be a penitent sinner. What she did to him was an expression of her great love to her Saviour, by whom her sins were forgiven.
>
> … therefore she loved much; for it is plain, by the tenor of Christ's discourse, that *the loving much was not the cause, but the effect, of her pardon,* and of her comfortable sense of it; for *we love God because he first loved us; he did not forgive us because we first loved him."*[48]

[48] https://www.biblestudytools.com/commentaries/matthew-henry-complete/luke/7.html - Accessed 24/01/2022

The evidence produced thus far, points to the truth that God's forgiveness of the sinner is inextricably linked to repentance. The apostle John, therefore, who sat under the teaching of Jesus himself, and who was subsequently baptised with the spirit of truth, is able to declare with unquestionable authority when he writes: "*If we confess our sins*, He is faithful and just to forgive us our sins and to cleanse us from all unrighteousness."

Chapter Seven

God's Justice Denied

One morning a lady visited the Christian bookshop where I have the privilege of working as a volunteer on a part-time basis. After browsing through the books in the children's section for a short while, she approached the counter and asked if we stocked any children's books on the "Easter Story," by which of course she meant the crucifixion and resurrection. Not being aware of anything off the top of my head, I too began to browse through the children's books. Unsurprisingly, there was no shortage of titles which covered the classic Old Testament Bible stories from creation to the flood, not to mention the many famous Bible characters from antiquity including Abraham, Joseph, Moses, and King David. Suffice to say, the shop was also amply stocked with books on the life, ministry, and works of our Lord Jesus, along with the journeys and experiences of the first-century apostles; but alas, nothing at all was to be found that dealt with, what the customer had referred to as, the "Easter Story."

After the lady had left the shop empty-handed, the thought struck me that I had never really come across a children's book which dealt with the crucifixion. Now while I'm not saying such books are non-existent, it would be fair to say that they are indeed thin on the ground. Upon further reflection, I concluded that this scenario was hardly surprising given that it would be difficult to produce a *cuddly* child-friendly version of the crucifixion. After all, it is a story full of betrayal, brutality, untold suffering, and even murder, not subjects suitable to be aired before the children's 9 pm watershed on TV, so to speak.

Sadly however, an aversion to the more unpalatable aspects of the crucifixion, I would suggest, is not only evident among the writers of Children's Bible story books, but is also evident among the sermons of many Ministers and Pastors who tend to avoid such contentious issues for fear of offending those more sensitive souls in their respective congregations. While many will labour on the love of God, the counterbalance evident in the justice of a Holy and righteous God, tends to be downplayed, if not eliminated. As I will seek to explain, such an approach has a direct effect on the understanding of forgiveness. When we neglect the doctrine of Penal Substitution, i.e., the view that our Lord Jesus actually paid the price for our sin in order that those who believe could be declared righteous, we end up with the distorted view that a "loving God" freely forgiving sin unconditionally, with the result that this distorted teaching is presented as the example Christians are to follow.

One modern-day theologian who promotes such a view is Steve Chalke. Writing in his book, "The Lost Message of Jesus" (2003), Chalke declares that the Bible "never defines Him [God] as anything other than love," and that "everything is to be tempered, interpreted, understood and seen through the one, primary lens of God's love."[49] In downplaying the view that God is also pictured as a judge who administers divine justice, it is not surprising therefore that Chalke denies the doctrine of Penal Substitution. In presenting his particular interpretation of John 3:16, Chalke therefore asserts:

> "John's Gospel famously declares, *"God loved the people of this world so much that he gave his only Son"* (John 3:16). How then, have we come to believe that at the cross this God of love suddenly decides to vent his anger and wrath on his own son? The fact is [Chalke continues] the cross isn't a form of cosmic child abuse – a vengeful Father, punishing his son for an offence he has not even committed."[50]

---

[49] Steve Chalke, *The Lost Message of Jesus* (Zondervan, Grand Rapids, Michigan, 2003), 63.
[50] Ibid., 182.

Rather, Steve Chalke proposes that on the cross, Jesus "absorbed all the pain, all the suffering caused by the breakdown in our relationship with God, and in doing so demonstrated the lengths to which a God who is 'love' will go to restore it."[51] This *user-friendly* or *easy believism* version of the crucifixion teaches that Christ's death on the cross was purely an act of love on His part, in the *hope* that such a demonstration of love would melt the hearts of sinful men and women and in so doing bring them to faith in Jesus.

Before proceeding to delve a little further into the doctrine of the atonement, which respected twentieth-century theologian, Louis Berkhof, declares is often called, "The heart of the gospel,"[52] it is perhaps needful to pause for a moment and ponder the advice which Berkhof proffers:

> "It is necessary to avoid all one-sidedness in this respect. If we represent the atonement as found only in the righteousness and justice of God, we fail to do justice to the love of God as a moving cause of the atonement. ... If on the other hand, we consider the atonement purely as an expression of the love of God, we fail to do justice to the righteousness and veracity of God, and we reduce the sufferings and the death of Christ to an unexplained enigma."[53]

With this principle in mind, Berkhof also cautions: "God cannot simply be compared to a private individual, who can without injustice forget about personal grievances." God, Berkhof continues, "is the judge of all the earth, and in that capacity must maintain the law and exercise strict justice." A judge, Berkhof concludes, "may be very kind-hearted, generous, and forgiving as a private individual, but in his official capacity he must see to it that the law takes its course."[54]

Turning to scripture it is evident that God's eternal plan of redemption was to culminate in God Himself taking on human flesh in the form

---

[51]Ibid., 181.
[52]Louis Berkhof, *Systematic Theology* (The Banner of Truth Trust, Edinburgh, 1994), 367.
[53]Ibid., 368.
[54]Ibid., 371.

of His Son, who would suffer willingly as a substitute for sinners. We see this truth plainly set forth in 2 Corinthians 5:21, which reads:

"For He made Him who knew no sin to be sin for us, that we might become the righteousness of God in Him." Commenting on this passage, John MacArthur, in his book "The Murder of Jesus," writes: "In other words, on the cross, God imputed our sin to Christ and then punished Him for it...The holy Son of God who had never known even the most insignificant sin would become sin – an object of God's fury."[55] Later on in his book, MacArthur again references 2 Corinthians 5:21 and addresses "religious liberals" specifically when he states:

> "As Christ hung there, He was bearing the sins of the world. He was dying as a substitute for others. To Him was imputed the guilt of their sins and He was suffering the punishment for those sins on their behalf. And the very essence of that punishment was the outpouring of God's wrath against sinners. In some mysterious way during those awful hours on the cross, the Father poured out the full measure of His wrath against sin and the recipient of that wrath was God's own beloved Son!
>
> In this lies the true meaning of the cross. Those who try to explain the atoning work of Christ in any other terms inevitably end up nullifying the truth of Christ's atonement altogether."[56]

Thus, it wasn't vengeance that the Father was heaping upon Christ on the cross, it was *justice*; the just penalty demanded by a Holy God for the law we had broken as a consequence of our rebellion. The correct picture, therefore, is presented by John Stott when he describes what he terms, "the self-substitution of God,"[57] in that a Holy and Just God pays the sin debt, and takes upon himself the punishment due for our sin.

---

[55] John MacArthur, *The Murder of Jesus* (Thomas Nelson Inc., Nashville, Tennessee, 2004) 71 & 73.
[56] Ibid., 218-219.
[57] John R.W. Stott, *The Cross of Christ* (Downs Grove, IL, Intervarsity Press, 1986), 133.

While it must be pointed out that not all those theologians who promote unconditional forgiveness, agree with Steve Chalke's views on the crucifixion, I still propose that the downplaying of the justice of God in any shape or form within the doctrine of the atonement, inevitability leads to a distorted view of repentance in general. For example, Steve Chalke heaps scorn on the Pharisees, Israel's first-century religious leaders, and states that they, "had a very simple message for you: "Repent! Purify yourself in order to make yourself socially and religiously acceptable."[58] In light of this statement, it seems to have escaped Steve Chalke that in Acts 2:38, we find the Apostle Peter declaring basically the same message as the Pharisees when he declares: "*Repent, and be baptized every one of you in the name of Jesus Christ for the remission of sins.*" It is not surprising therefore that later on in his book, Chalke again appears to contradict the Apostle Peter's teaching that repentance and baptism must precede the "remission of sins" when on the contrary, Chalke rather declares: "acceptance precedes repentance – not the other way round."[59]

Finally, as regards Steve Chalke's particular take on repentance itself, in accepting that "Jesus often used the word *repent*" (Matthew 4:17; Mark 1:15), Chalke seeks to redefine repentance in a much more user-friendly way by declaring that it's simply about "living your life differently….a call to a new agenda, a different way of doing life."[60] Thus Chalke concludes, "somewhere along the line we have fundamentally misunderstood what He [Jesus] was saying and turned it [repentance] from a positive to a negative." As a consequence [Chalke continues] "Repentance has become an often quoted but little understood term."[61]

The outworking of the stance adopted by Chalke, and indeed liberal theologians in general, is that in seeking to reinterpret repentance in a more modern light, they are inadvertently downplaying sin, or to be a little more specific, the quilt of sin. In admonishing such a view, John Stott issues this sobering statement:

---

[58]Steve Chalke, *The Lost Message of Jesus,* 87.
[59]Ibid., 99.
[60]Steve Chalke, *The Lost Message of Jesus,* 116.
[61]Ibid., 116.

"The practice of covering or concealing sin is characteristic of unbelievers. They neither acknowledge their sins nor feel their guilt or peril. Consequently, they do not cry to God to have mercy on them or flee to Jesus Christ for refuge from the judgement their sins deserve. Indeed, this old-fashioned language means nothing to them. If they heard it, they would laugh at it. But their position is far more serious than they realize. "Whoever conceals their sins does not prosper." They are on the broad road which leads to destruction."[62]

Here then is one of the primary obstacles to correctly understanding biblical forgiveness. While some theologians like Steve Chalke seem to minimise sin and repentance, asserting that the Kingdom of God is "a Kingdom of inclusion and acceptance,"[63] others like Jay Adams (rightly in my view) point out that, "Acceptance is a non-judgemental reception of a person as he is, [which] amounts to condoning sin. Forgiveness, on the contrary, judges each one, calling sin "sin" refusing to condone sin or ignore it but gladly forgiving it on repentance."[64] Concluding on the crucifixion therefore, I fully concur again with John Stott when he writes:

"When we look at the cross we see the justice, love, wisdom and power of God. It is not easy to decide which is the most luminously revealed, whether the justice of God in judging sin, or the love of God in bearing the judgment in our place, or the wisdom of God in perfectly combining the two, or the power of God in saving those who believe. For the cross is equally an act, and therefore a demonstration, of God's justice, love, wisdom and power. The cross assures us that this God is the reality within, behind and beyond the universe."[65]

---

[62]John Stott, *Confess Your Sins, The Way of Reconciliation* (Eerdmans Publishing Co. Grand Rapids, Michigan, 2017), 7.
[63]Steve Chalke, *The Lost Message of Jesus*, 28.
[64]Jay Adams, *From Forgiven to Forgiving*, 112.
[65]John Stott, *The Cross of Christ* (Inter-Varsity Press, Leister, England, 2006), 274.

Repentance is Essential

Reference was made earlier to Jesus' prayer on the cross, and the apostle Stephen's dying petition, and in particular that these statements should be understood in light of what I termed, "the Biblical criteria for forgiveness." It is also important to bear in mind, that both these accounts are framed within the "vertical" realm, namely God's dealing with sinful humanity. In order therefore to grasp the real significance of Jesus' prayer, and Stephen's dying petition, it must be further asserted that God's justice demands repentance before forgiveness can be granted, whereupon the sinner is saved from the penalty of sin and declared righteous. To reiterate the point I made earlier, when both Jesus and Stephen asked God to grant forgiveness, in effect what they were requesting was that sinners would be drawn to a recognition of their sin, leading to repentance and faith. Again, it is simply inconceivable that a God of justice would present a particular pathway to salvation through the teaching of Jesus, only to abandon the core principle of repentance within that process.

For example, Jesus proclaims in Luke 5:32: *"I have not come to call the righteous, but sinners, to repentance."* In Mark 1:14-15 we read that, *"Jesus came to Galilee, preaching the gospel of the kingdom of God, and saying, "The time is fulfilled, and the kingdom of God is at hand. Repent, and believe in the gospel."* Then in Luke 24:47, Jesus lays out the mission of the New Testament Church when He declares, *"that repentance and remission of sins should be preached in His name to all nations, beginning at Jerusalem."* And in direct fulfilment of this command, we read throughout the book of Acts that repentance was indeed central to the Christian message. In Acts 2:38, we see the apostle Peter declaring, *"Repent, and let every one of you be baptized in the name of Jesus Christ for the remission of sins; and you shall receive the gift of the Holy Spirit."* And again, Peter instructs his hearers in Acts 3:19 to, *"Repent therefore and be converted, that your sins may be blotted out, so that times of refreshing may come from the presence of the Lord."* (Also see Acts 17:30; 20:21; 26:20; 1 John 1:9)

While many more biblical examples could be cited from other New Testament sources, based on what we have examined already there can be no doubt that when it comes to God's relationship with sinful humanity, and particularly in regards to the Christian believer passing from "death to life," heartfelt repentance is central and indeed an essential part of that process.

When the Lord brought me to faith following a series of events in 1998, the first thing I did on bended knee was to confess my sin before God. Having seldom if ever attended a church in the previous twenty years, it was not as if I had been well-versed in what was expected. Rather, having been brought to an increasing awareness of my sinful lifestyle and having helplessly, as it were, fallen upon Jesus, I can only conclude that it was my Saviour who brought me through the process of repentance leading to saving faith.

That said however, it is important to clarify the standing of the believer in the world we live in, and point out that we are soberly reminded in 1 John 1:8: *"If we say that we have no sin, we deceive ourselves, and the truth is not in us."* The truth revealed in Scripture is that while the Christian believer will grow in maturity and learn to shun wilful sin. The fact remains that as they still maintain, what the Bible refers to as a *fleshly* (or human) nature (Galatians 5:17), Christians remain susceptible to sin daily, through thought, word and deed. Dealing with these *daily trespasses,* therefore, will form the basis of our next chapter as we seek to broaden our study, and in so doing, examine the role of forgiveness in man's ongoing relationship with his fellow man.

Chapter Eight

Forgiving One Another

We now move into the realm of the "horizontal" dimension of biblical forgiveness, namely the role forgiveness has to play in the believer's relationships with fellow believers, and others within the wider society. The title of this book therefore, "Forgiveness Through The Lens Of Heaven" was deliberately chosen, as I intend to examine the nature of genuine biblical forgiveness which has the potential to bear fruit, i.e., forgiveness which produces true and lasting reconciliation in the society in which we live. All too often, a simplistic view of forgiveness is presented today which places all the onus on the one who has been wronged to forgive unconditionally, regardless of the seriousness of the offence. To quote a recently published work which is relevant to our overall study, titled, "Considering Grace" (which was produced by the Presbyterian Church in Ireland to document the experiences of some of its parishioners during the Northern Ireland conflict) a contributor named Isobel declares: "We are called to forgive even though you've been the victim of injustice and even though those who have done you this injustice are not repenting, or don't even perceive they have done you an injustice."[66]

While I accept that the contributors to the aforementioned book were given the freedom to articulate their respective views, and while the authors did make reference to the fact that differing opinions were

---

[66]Gladys Ganiel & Jamie Yohanis, *Considering Grace Presbyterians And The Troubles* (Merrion Press, Co. Kildare, Ireland, 2019), 162.

expressed in relation to forgiveness and reconciliation,[67] the views expressed by Isobel, I contend, are a contradiction of God's model for forgiveness. This particular approach does little if anything to achieve a successful outcome, primarily that of true reconciliation. When we bear in mind that effectual forgiveness is an essential aspect of restoring any relationship, seeking to do so in circumstances where the offender refuses to take part in the process, is as pointless as shaking hands with yourself. This questionable approach to forgiveness and reconciliation is also apparent in the writings of R.T. Kendal when he declares:

> ".... reconciliation is not always essential to [what Kendal defines as] total forgiveness. It takes place in the heart; one does not need to know whether one's enemy will reconcile. If I have forgiven him or her in my heart of hearts, and he doesn't want to speak to me, I can still have the victory. It is true that it is easier to forgive when I know that those who maligned or betrayed us are sorry; but if I must have this before I can forgive, I may never have the victory."[68]

Again, it is difficult to see how such an approach will produce any reconciliation, which itself is the true goal of Biblical forgiveness. As previously pointed out, the Apostle Paul presents a clear picture of true forgiveness and teaches that no one is forgiven by God, without being reconciled to God (2 Corinthians 5:17-21). Ultimately therefore, the problem with what R.T. Kendal defines here as "forgiveness…in the heart", and which Timothy Keller refers to as "inner forgiveness," is that such "forgiveness" will seldom, if ever, produce a satisfactory outcome as regards lasting reconciliation between the parties involved. Yes indeed, the believer must seek to nurture within his or her heart a *willingness to forgive*, as and when the appropriate circumstances are met. But in this instance, there is a vast difference between being willing to do something and being in a position to do it.

---

[67] Ibid., 47.
[68] R.T. Kendall, *Total Forgiveness*, 32-33.

In promoting unconditional forgiveness, June Hunt also facilitates this problematic scenario when she writes: "Forgiveness requires no relationship" and as such, "Forgiveness can take place with only one person."[69] Again, I can only conclude that such a view is at variance with God's model, as it is evident throughout the Scriptures that divine forgiveness does not end with the pardon of sin, but rather, having been declared righteous, we begin a new relationship with God. American theologian, L. Gregory Jones, writes: "People are mistaken if they think of Christian forgiveness primarily as absolution from guilt; the purpose of forgiveness is the restoration of communion, the reconciliation of brokenness."[70] And, Chris Brauns adds: "God's forgiveness is inextricably linked to reconciliation. No one is forgiven by God without being reconciled to God."[71] By way of substantiating this position, Brauns explains how the apostle Paul interchangeably refers to the gospel as both "the forgiveness of sins" (Colossians 1:14, cf. Ephesians 1:7), and "the ministry of reconciliation" (2 Corinthians 5:17-21).[72] For effectual forgiveness to mean anything, therefore, it must open the door to reconciliation.

A Model for Conflict Resolution

As an example of the lengths Jesus would have us go to in order to restore broken relationships and achieve true reconciliation, we turn to the gospel of Matthew, chapter 18, where our Lord lays out a four-point plan as a model for conflict resolution. Discipline, and more importantly, a model for administering discipline, is essential in any environment, particularly within the faith community. Human nature alone dictates that there will be times when an offence cannot simply be overlooked. Within the faith community, therefore, such sin must be addressed if it is likely to bring dishonour upon God, and by implication cause others to think less of His infallible Word. And of course, there is nothing

---

[69]June Hunt, *Forgiveness The Freedom To Let Go* (Hendrickson Publishers, Massachusetts, USA, 2013), 18.
[70]Chris Brauns, *Unpacking Forgiveness* (Crossway, Wheaton, Illinois, 2008), 48.
[71]Ibid., 48
[72]Ibid., 48-49.

more likely to cause someone to stumble than to witness unaddressed sin and the conflict which ensues within the church environment. To this end, the four-stage model for *church discipline* as laid out by Jesus in Matthew 18:15-17 could not be any clearer:

> *"Moreover if your brother sins against you, go and tell him his fault between you and him alone. If he hears you, you have gained your brother. But if he will not hear, take with you one or two more, that 'by the mouth of two or three witnesses every word may be established.' And if he refuses to hear them, tell it to the church. But if he refuses even to hear the church, let him be to you like a heathen and a tax collector."*

The first stage of the process is relatively simple. If someone has been offended, they go to the offender and openly discuss the matter, making known their fault. This command aligns perfectly with a similar instruction pertaining to the resolution of disputes also given by Jesus, as recorded in Luke 17:3: *"Take heed to yourselves. If your brother sins against you, rebuke him; and if he repents, forgive him."* Regrettably, however, the apparent contradiction in Timothy Keller's teaching as regards forgiveness becomes only too evident here again. In commenting on this first stage of the reconciliation process in Matthew 18:15-17, Keller recommends that "we must forgive inwardly…before we go ask the wrongdoer to repent. If you go to the perpetrator *before* you forgive them, you are likely to go not to regain your brother or sister."[73]

Again, I can only conclude that the correct attitude must be to go with a *willingness to forgive*, when and if the circumstances are met by way of repentance on the part of the wrongdoer. As we will see, this is clearly the sentiment underpinning the entire process. The motivation for this first stage of the process, and the tact with which it is handled therefore, is of vital importance. John MacArthur offers worthy advice when he writes:

---

[73]Timothy Keller, Forgive Why Should I And How Can I? 188.

"The goal of church discipline is not to throw people out, shun them, embarrass them, or to be self-righteous, play God, or exercise authority in an abusive or dictatorial manner. The purpose of discipline is to bring people back into a right relationship with God and with the rest of the body. Proper discipline is never administered as retaliation for someone's sin. Restoration, not retribution, is always the goal."[74]

Ken Sande strikes a similar note as regards this first stage of the process of reconciliation. By highlighting the context of the passage in question, Sande refers to the preceding verses in Matthew 18, and points out that here, "we find Jesus' wonderful metaphor of a loving shepherd who goes back for a wandering sheep and then rejoices when it is found." Thus, Sande concludes, "Matthew 18:15 is introduced with a theme of restoration, not condemnation."[75]

The apostle Paul, when writing to believers, also presents the correct attitude which should be adopted when confronting someone about a transgression: *"Brethren, if a man is overtaken in any trespass, you who are spiritual restore such a one in a spirit of gentleness, considering yourself lest you also be tempted. Bear one another's burdens, and so fulfil the law of Christ"* (Galatians 6:1-2). Having approached an offending brother therefore, whereupon he "hears" you and repents, the offended party is to forgive, reconciliation takes place, and the matter is closed.

If, however, the offender does not admit any wrongdoing, the second stage in the process is to return again to speak with him, this time in the presence of one or two neutral witnesses who are in a position to listen to the evidence, and counsel accordingly. If, after this second meeting, the offender accepts that he has been in the wrong, forgiveness is granted, reconciliation takes place, and the issue goes no further. If the offender, however, still maintains his innocence, the third stage involves formally bringing the matter before the representatives of the church.

---

[74]John F. MacArthur, *The Freedom and Power of Forgiveness* (Crossway Books, Wheaton, Illinois, USA, 1999), 141.
[75]Ken Sande, *The Peace Maker*, 144.

If at this juncture, the offender now begins to recognise the seriousness of his actions, whereupon there is a change of heart and repentance is forthcoming, forgiveness is granted, and the matter is closed.

Finally, in the event that after all these negotiations, the offender has not accepted any wrongdoing, and still refuses to repent, stage four of the process states that he is to be treated *"as a Gentile [unbeliever] and a tax collector."* (ESV) By way of explanation concerning the implications of this final course of action, Ken Sande writes:

> "Jesus' use of the word *as* is significant" here in Matthew 18:17, pointing out that, "Since only God can know a person's heart (1 Samuel 16:7; Revelation 2:23), the church has no power to decide whether a person is a believer. Instead, the church is called only to make a functional decision: If a person behaves like a nonbeliever would – by disregarding the authority of scripture and of Christ's church – he should be treated as if he were a nonbeliever."[76]

While such a move would initially involve the removal of various membership privileges like communion, and positions of leadership or teaching, Ken Sande again offers caution when he adds: "treating others as unbelievers also means that we look for every opportunity to evangelize them: We [continue to] remind them again and again of the good news of salvation through Jesus Christ and urge them to receive his forgiveness by repenting and turning from their sin."[77]

While to some, such a move seems harsh, particularly in light of the prevailing sensitivities which abound today, it is nonetheless a well-established biblical principle designed to maintain the purity and integrity of the Church Body. For example, in 1 Corinthians 5:13, believers are urged to *"put away from yourselves the evil person,"* and again, with a view to exercising discipline, the apostle Paul instructs Timothy to rebuke sin *"in the presence of all, that the rest also may fear"* (1 Timothy 5:20).

[76]Ibid., 193.
[77]Ibid., 194

While of course, this process relates primarily to church discipline, and specifically, as has been stated, to maintaining the integrity and purity of the Body, there are nonetheless practical principles which are relevant concerning the broader application of forgiveness and reconciliation. As Chris Brauns points out, "It is a mistake to think of these verses as applying only to church discipline. The principles of these verses can be applied to other relationships as well."[78]

In applying these principles to wider society, therefore, the glaring question which presents itself is, where within this process is there any justification for the view that, to quote again the aforementioned contributor to "Considering Grace," "We are called to forgive even though you've been the victim of injustice and even though those who have done you this injustice are not repenting?"[79] The fact of the matter is, if forgiveness were to be administered unconditionally on every occasion where we have been wronged, this entire model is unworkable. Jay E. Adams comments on the process outlined in Matthew 18:15-17:

> *"If we were to grant forgiveness to a brother apart from his repentance and desire for forgiveness, then why bother with the process?* One would simply say, "I forgive you" and walk away. The whole point of the progressive nature of Christ's programme of discipline is that where there is no repentance, increasingly larger efforts must be made to bring it about. The matter cannot be dropped simply by saying, "I forgive you, whether you repent or not." God is not interested in forgiveness as an end in itself, or as a therapeutic technique that benefits the one doing the forgiving. He wants reconciliation to take place, and that can only be brought about by repentance."[80]

---

[78]Chris Brauns, *Unpacking Forgiveness* (Crossway, Wheaton, Illinois, 2008), 106.
[79]Gladys Ganiel & Jamie Yohanis, *Considering Grace Presbyterians And The Troubles* (Merrion Press, Co. Kildare, Ireland, 2019), 162.
[80]Jay E. Adams, *From Forgiven to Forgiving* (Calvary Press, Amityville, NY, 1994), 33.

There is, however, another principle evident both within this process, and within the other passage referred to above (Luke 17:3), that is to say, when we wish to seek reconciliation with an offender, the first thing we are to do is "go and tell him his fault," and what's more, if the offender refuses to repent, we are not to shy away from raising the matter when appropriate, again and again. And yet, it is this vital aspect of conflict resolution which is so often omitted today by those who would seek to follow an easier path and promote unconditional forgiveness rather than confront an unrepentant offender.

In conclusion, therefore, there will be times when it is legitimate to conclude that, outside of an intervention by the Holy Spirit in converting the heart of the offender, there are times when forgiveness and reconciliation are not possible. In short, there are times when the offended party, in faith, must leave the matter in the hands of the Lord (Romans 12:19) and move on. While I appreciate that such a scenario raises a great many issues, not least the allegation that such a course of action inevitably leads to the harbouring of animosities which in the long term can prove damaging to the offended party, I propose to show later on, that such an outcome need not be inevitable. Indeed, I intend to present a biblical pathway by which those who have suffered injustice, can in time, come to live fulfilled lives even in the shadow of unresolved conflict. To proceed along that path, we continue to examine how God's example of forgiveness should impact our attitude to the healing of wounds, and relationship building.

Chapter Nine

Forgive as God Forgives

Two specific texts which again speak directly and plainly about believer's responsibilities regarding forgiveness, are found in Ephesians 4:31-32, and Colossians 3:12-13. First, the apostle Paul, writing to the church at Ephesus declares: *"Let all bitterness, wrath, anger, clamor, and evil speaking be put away from you, with all malice. And be kind to one another, tenderhearted, forgiving one another,* **just as God in Christ forgave you.** *"* And again, Paul writes in a similar vein to the Colossian believers: *"Therefore, as the elect of God, holy and beloved, put on tender mercies, kindness, humility, meekness, long-suffering; bearing with one another, and forgiving one another, if anyone has a complaint against another; even as Christ forgave you, so you also must do."* A common theme in both these passages is that believers are to exercise forgiveness in the same way as God in Christ forgives them. Chris Brauns explains:

> "God expects Christians to forgive one another in the same way that He forgives them. The Bible teaches us that God's forgiveness is a commitment by the one true God to pardon graciously those who repent and believe so that they are reconciled to Him and will one day be glorified. This serves as the blueprint for how all forgiveness should take place."[81]

Problems arise, however, when scholars ignore the principles laid down

---

[81]Chris Brauns, *Unpacking Forgiveness* (Crossway, Wheaton, Illinois, 2008), 52.

in those passages which we have already examined, namely Matthew 18:15-17, which dealt with Church discipline, and Luke 17:3 which reads: *"If your brother sins against you, rebuke him; and if he repents, forgive him."* Having done so, they further compound their error by declaring that we are to *forgive as God forgives*, based on erroneous interpretations of Christ's prayer on the cross, the apostle Stephen's dying petition, and the accounts of the paralytic man and the sinful woman. In conclusion therefore they state that, as Jesus forgave those who never repented, then likewise, believers should forgive without any preconditions.

On the contrary, however, having deduced in our studies thus far that neither Jesus nor Stephen, forgave anyone unconditionally, and in light of the plain teaching of Scripture texts previously quoted which confirm the necessity of repentance (particularly as we will see later, for those sins which cannot be overlooked in love), I can only conclude that the apostle Paul here in Ephesians and Colossians is instructing believers to exercise forgiveness in like manner. Referencing Ephesians 4:32 specifically, Jay Adams also comments:

> "It should go without saying that since our forgiveness is modelled after God's (Ephesians 4:32), it must be conditional. Forgiveness by God rests on clear, unmistakable conditions. The apostles did not merely announce that God had forgiven men, who should acknowledge and rejoice the fact but, rather, they were sent forth to preach *"repentance and the forgiveness of sins"* (Luke 24:47; Acts 17:30). The sins of those who repented and trusted in the Saviour as the One who shed His blood for them were forgiven *on the conditions of repentance and faith.*"

That said, however, it is important to recognise at this juncture, that in both these passages, Ephesians 4:31-32, and Colossians 3:12-13, the clear emphasis is very much on the forgiver, and in particular, the role forgiveness plays in maintaining good relationships marked by, *kindness, humility, meekness,* and *long-suffering,* as opposed to contentious relationships marked with *bitterness, anger,* and *evil speaking.* With this thought in mind, therefore, it is important to note that the issues around repentance, forgiveness, and reconciliation, are often more complex than they would first appear. These aspects will be examined further in chapter twelve.

Forgive us Our Debts.

In Matthew 6:9-13, Jesus presents a model prayer for believers which includes the following petition: *"Forgive us our debts, as we forgive our debtors"* (v 12). It is also worth noting that in a footnote to the Lord's Prayer, the importance of forgiveness is highlighted again when Our Lord elaborates: *"For if you forgive men their trespasses, your heavenly Father will also forgive you. But if you do not forgive men their trespasses, neither will your Father forgive your trespasses"* (Verses 14-15). This passage also is frequently misused by those who would promote unconditional forgiveness. In quoting this extract from the Lord's Prayer, again, in light of an erroneous interpretation of Jesus petition on the cross, it is asserted that Christians should forgive unconditionally, otherwise God will not forgive them. However, such a stance even falls foul of the teaching within the above passage itself. On one hand, it is stated that Christians should follow God's example and forgive *unconditionally*, while on the other hand, it is said that God's forgiveness of those who fail to forgive, is in fact, *conditional*.

In order to bring some clarity, there are several points which must be addressed. First, it is necessary to familiarise ourselves with the various processes in the life journey of the Christian believer. The Bible teaches that having been "justified" by God's grace, the remainder of the believer's life is one of "sanctification." Now I'm aware that these terms may be unfamiliar to the reader, so in an attempt to simplify matters, could I suggest that the process goes something like this; Having been given the gift of faith (Ephesians 2:8), and by implication adopted into God's family, for the remainder of their lives, Christian believers go through a process of sanctification as they continue to grow in faith by way of studying the Scriptures, engaging in prayer, and worshipping together with like-minded believers under the preaching of God's word. In light of this process therefore, it must also be recognised that as God administers forgiveness in the world, He does so in two distinct capacities; First as a judge presiding over wider humanity, and secondly, as a loving Father disciplining, or sanctifying, His children. Pastor John MacArthur elaborates:

> "…. divine forgiveness has two aspects. One is the *judicial forgiveness* God grants as Judge. This is the forgiveness that was purchased by the atonement Christ rendered on our behalf. This kind of forgiveness frees us from any threat of eternal condemnation. It is the forgiveness of justification. Such pardon is immediately complete and never needs to be sought again. The other is a *parental forgiveness* God grants as our Father. He is grieved when His children sin. The forgiveness of justification takes care of judicial guilt, but it does not nullify His fatherly displeasure over our sin. He chastens those whom He loves, for their temporal good (Hebrews 12:5-10). So the forgiveness Christians are supposed to seek in their daily walk is not pardon from an angry judge, but mercy from a grieved Father."[82]

It should also be emphasised that this teaching is not some recent development within Christian theology, but was taught many years ago in the Westminster Confession of Faith, which declares: "God doth continue to forgive the sins of those who are justified; and although they can never fall from the state of justification: yet they may, by their sins, fall under His fatherly displeasure."[83]

With this distinction now in mind, we note again that it is not the salvation, or to be more precise, the justification of the believer which is in focus here in the Lord's Prayer. Rather, as previously stated, this is

---

[82]John McArthur, *The Freedom and Power of Forgiveness* (Crossway Books, Wheaton, Illinois, USA, 1999), 58.
[83]Westminster Confession Of Faith, *Chapter XI. Of Justification,* Paragraph V.

a prayer for Christian believers, as evidenced by the fact that it is only believers who can rightly refer to God as, "Our Father". The "debts," or sins referred to in the Lord's Prayer, are those daily transgressions committed by a Christian, and in particular, the sin associated with an *unforgiving spirit*. It is accepted therefore that, at times, God may deem it necessary to discipline His children, in the same way a loving parent will from time to time feel it necessary to reprimand a wayward child. Hebrews 12:6-10, referenced by MacArthur, presents this truth:

> *"For whom the Lord loves He chastens.... God deals with you as with sons; for what son is there whom a father does not chasten?.... Furthermore, we have had human fathers who corrected us, and we paid them respect. Shall we not much more readily be in subjection to the Father of spirits and live? For they indeed for a few days chastened us as seemed best to them, but He for our profit, that we may be partakers of His holiness."[84]*

Concerning God's parental discipline, Chris Brauns states: "If you are a believer, the purpose of God's discipline is not to inflict upon you the punishment you deserve [but rather] God disciplines his children so they will understand the seriousness of sin and will increasingly conform to the image of his Son."[85] In correctly stating that while "Salvation is unconditional; fellowship with the Father is conditional," R.T. Kendal writes: "fellowship with the Father on our way to heaven is conditional, because we may temporarily lose fellowship with the Father." This scenario, Kendal elaborates, could manifest itself when, "the power of the holy spirit in our lives – may ebb and flow."[86]

By way of a biblical example pertaining to how God disciplines His children, we turn to the often-chaotic life of King David. During that period after David had sinned with Bathsheba, and before his sin was revealed, and he was subsequently humbled before God, David writes of that time in his life when his inner peace was taken away: *"When I*

---

[84] John McArthur, *The Freedom and Power of Forgiveness*, 59-60.
[85] Chris Brauns, *Unpacking Forgiveness* (Crossway, Wheaton, Illinois, 2008), 50-51.
[86] R.T. Kendal, *Total Forgiveness*, 78.

kept silent, my bones grew old through my groaning all the day long. For day and night Your hand was heavy upon me; My vitality was turned into the drought of summer" (Psalm 32:3-4).

It is clear, therefore, that the subject of forgiveness here in the Lord's Prayer, pertains *not just* to the relationship between the believer and God, but equally to the relationship between believers themselves, and indeed the wider community. The lesson we learn from this passage is quite simple; if the believer does not display a forgiving spirit in general towards those around them, then God as a loving Father, is justified in chastening His children to teach them a vital lesson. The Christian believer, therefore, should consider very carefully the full implication when praying these words: "Forgive us our debts, as we forgive our debtors," not least because, again as has been highlighted, Jesus unequivocally goes on to condemn an unforgiving spirit when He states: *"But if you do not forgive men their trespasses, neither will your Father forgive your trespasses"* (verses 14-15). In other words, for as long as the Christian *unjustly* withholds forgiveness towards others, so their Father will withhold forgiveness and its accompanying blessing, from the believer.

However, lest confusion may creep in at this point, please note carefully my emphasis above on, *"unjustly"* withholding forgiveness. While, as has been pointed out, there are occasions when the believer is perfectly justified in denying forgiveness to an offender (Matthew 18:17), there are nonetheless, also very clear guidelines about circumstances where it is wrong, and even sinful to unjustly withhold forgiveness from others.

Chapter Ten

When to Forgive

One of the greatest challenges that presents itself when studying the subject of forgiveness is that we are called to self-examination, and in particular we are drawn to ask the question, "What are my real motives and desires towards those who have wronged me?" Very often, the answer to that question may seem too difficult to contemplate, with the result that the subject of forgiveness is simply avoided. It is hoped, however, that as we delve a little further into the subject, some of those fears may be alleviated as it becomes clear what the restoration of broken relationships might entail for all concerned.

It is also the case that when someone thinks of forgiveness, they wrongly imagine that to forgive someone simply means letting them off. However, I quote again Gregory Jones when he writes, "People are mistaken if they think of Christian forgiveness primarily as absolution from guilt; the purpose of forgiveness is the restoration of communion, the reconciliation of brokenness."[87] To be able to get from a position of mistrust and even animosity, which characterises many broken relationships, to a point where reconciliation is a reality, requires extraordinary strength and commitment on both sides. While it is my intention to devote the remainder of the study to looking specifically at the obligations placed on the one who has been wronged and is therefore the one who may be asked to forgive, there is one important question that needs to be answered from this perspective: "How do I recognise when someone is truly repentant of past actions?"

---

[87]Chris Brauns, *Unpacking Forgiveness* (Crossway, Wheaton, Illinois, 2008), 48.

Genuine Repentance

Taking Luke 17:3 again as our starting point: "If your brother sins against you, rebuke him; and if he repents, forgive him," and with a view to looking more closely at those occasions when forgiveness should be granted, it is necessary first of all to take a moment and examine what *genuine repentance* might look like. John MacArthur, for example, declares: "Genuine repentance always involves a confession of wrongdoing and a willingness to make things right",[88] Chris Brauns elaborates a little further when he writes:

> "Biblically, to repent means to change behaviour as a result of a complete change of thinking and attitude. People in our culture sometimes limit repentance to an emotion, and certainly emotions should be included. But at its centre, to repent means to turn around in actions and attitude."[89]

Likewise, David Augsburger writes, repentance is "A change of mind and heart. It is necessary for release of guilt; more, it is the basis of right relations with God. In repentance, the heart is not only broken *for* its sins but from its sins."[90]

John Stott also highlights the necessary attitude that must accompany genuine repentance and, in so doing, brings another dimension into view when he writes: "It is not enough to confess [our sins], asking for forgiveness and cleansing; we need deliberately, definitely, specifically to forsake them... and go on to adopt a right attitude towards both God and sin itself. ... The uncovering of sin is in itself of little value; it must lead us to an attitude both of humility towards God and of hostility towards sin."[91] While some might argue that bringing repentance before God into the equation places an unnecessary barrier in the way of an unbeliever who wishes to atone for a crime against someone, there is an important aspect of repentance which must be borne in mind. This relates to the *horizontal* and the *vertical* nature of sin itself. Jay Adams explains:

---

[88]John MacArthur, *The Freedom and Power of Forgiveness*, 185.
[89]Chris Brauns, *Unpacking Forgiveness*, 57.
[90]David Augsburger, *The new Freedom of Forgiveness*, 80.
[91]John Stott, *Confess Your Sins The Way of Reconciliation* (Eerdmans Publishing Co. Grand Rapids, Michigan, 2017), 12-13.

"Naturally, all sin, even against us (sin with a horizontal dimension), is also vertical (sin against God). This is because He has forbidden us to transgress against one another and commanded us rather to love and do good to one another. To do what God forbids or fail to do what He commands is sin against God."[92]

John MacArthur also highlights this reality when he states: "A sin against us always involves a greater sin against God,"[93] and as such, MacArthur concludes: "Even after we have forgiven offenders for their transgressions against us, God Himself may exact justice for their sins against Him. We can forgive an offence against us. But we cannot grant forgiveness for sin against God" (Luke 5:21).

Sadly, today, the concept of *repentance* itself has been all but been eliminated from secular vocabulary, and even within the so-called modern church, as I have already alluded, repentance is often downplayed. It is little wonder, therefore, that many have a flawed perception of what true repentance actually means, with the result that repenting today is regarded as little more than offering an apology. John MacArthur highlights the distinction: "Genuine repentance always involves a confession of wrongdoing and a willingness to make things right. An apology often takes the form of an excuse…. I'm sorry if you took offence, but…."[94] Addressing this same distinction between such an apology and genuine repentance, Ken Sande writes:

"To repent literally means to change the way we think…. It involves a waking up to the fact that we have been deceiving ourselves and that our ideas, attitudes, values, or goals have been wrong. If this change in thinking is genuine, it will lead to a renouncing of sin and a turning to God (Ezekiel 14:6; Acts 3:19)."[95]

---

[92]Jay E. Adams, *From Forgiven to Forgiving* (Calvary Press, Amityville, NY, 1994), 136.
[93]John MacArthur, *The Freedom and Power of Forgiveness* (Crossway Books, Wheaton, Illinois, USA, 1999), 84.
[94]Ibid., 185.
[95]Ken Sande, *The Peace Maker*, 118.

Ken Sande also produces a comprehensive seven-point guide called the Seven A's, which provide a framework for genuine repentance. Very briefly, the guidelines come under the following headings:

Address Everyone Involved

Generally speaking, the sin should be confessed to everyone who has been affected by the wrongdoing. As all sin is a violation against God, all sin should be confessed to Him (Psalm 32:5; 41:4).

Avoid If, But, and Maybe

Confession is not really confession if the desire is to shift the blame onto others, or if an attempt is made to minimise or excuse guilt. The most common way this takes place is when someone says, "I'm sorry *if* I've done something to offend." The word "if" nullifies any confession, as it infers that you do not know whether or not you did anything wrong at all. The same could be said of the word "but". When an offender says "I'm sorry, but…," the inference is that the words that precede "but" are superficial, whereas the words that follow reveal the offender's true attitude.

Admit Specifically

The more detailed and specific one is when making a confession, the more likely the response will be positive. Specific confessions help convince others that you are genuinely facing up to what you have done. Furthermore, being specific will help the offender identify any behavioural issues they may wish to change.

Acknowledge the Hurt

If, by confessing, the true desire is for a positive response, make a point of acknowledging remorse and sorrow for the hurt you have caused. It is important to show that you have genuine empathy for the other person's feelings as a consequence of your actions.

Accept the Consequences

Accepting any and all consequences for your actions is another way of demonstrating the genuineness of your confession. The prodigal son provides a demonstration of this principle, when, having been reunited with his father, he declares, *"I am no longer worthy to be called your son; make me like one of your hired hands"* (Luke 15:19).

Alter Your Behaviour

Sincere repentance is also marked by a desire to change your behaviour in the future. Personally, this could entail describing some of the attitudes, character traits, and behavioural patterns you hope to change with God's help.

Ask for Forgiveness (and Allow Time)

Having followed the six steps described, and as of yet, the person to whom you have confessed does not express forgiveness, you are now in a position to ask outright, "Will you please forgive me?" Sande cautions, however, that we should not use this question to pressurise someone, as some people can forgive quickly while others will need time to assess their feelings. Above all, Ken Sande concludes, when we go to confess a wrong, we should always bear in mind that we are serving the other person and not simply confessing to gain comfort for oneself.[96]

There is however, one addition I would suggest to the above list, and it relates to the specific nature and context of our overall study; that of civil conflict. John MacArthur highlights this important point: "The arena of the confession should be as large as the audience of the original offence. Public transgressions call for public confession."[97] Again, in light of the fact that the Northern Ireland conflict was played out in front of the world's media, and in many instances, deliberately so, it is only fitting and proper that any subsequent repentance for the crimes committed during that same conflict should address that same

---

[96]Ibid., 126-134
[97]John MacArthur, *The Freedom and Power of Forgiveness*, 185.

audience, not least with a view to stemming the flow of propaganda that is deliberately used to keep old animosities alive.

It is important, however, to bear in mind that the injured party must be careful not to place unachievable barriers in the way of the one requesting forgiveness. While it is very possible that there will be times when a request for forgiveness may prove less than authentic, it may be just as likely that we will reject a genuine penitent. David Augsburger cautions, therefore, that "the demand for an ironclad guarantee that will fix all future acts permanently and secure them from any future pain must be cancelled,"[98] and Ken Sande reminds us that "forgiveness is based on repentance, not on guarantees."[99] In effect, we are all human, and no one can make such a promise of perfection where the potential to fail and hurt someone again is ever present.

Finally, with a view to perhaps offering some solace to an offender who has come to regret his or her past actions, and who has struggled to deal with the lasting consequences, the writer to the Hebrews asks the following question: *"How much more shall the blood of Christ, who through the eternal Spirit offered Himself without spot to God,* **cleanse your conscience** *from dead works to serve the living God?" (Hebrews 9:14)*

Genuine Forgiveness

The cold hard truth is that we live in a world, where the concept of forgiveness is fast becoming less relevant in an increasingly secular environment. In this modern arena, some hold the view that forgiveness only encourages further lawlessness, while others will argue that to forgive only humanises perpetrators and makes it more difficult to hold them accountable. Such views are born of a mindset that declares that you can't have forgiveness and justice at the same time, in that these terms are seen as diametrically opposed to each other.

And this brings us back to the Christian worldview, and to the cross of Jesus Christ in particular, where, as we have already examined,

---

[98]David Augsburger, *The New Freedom of Forgiveness*, 50.
[99]Ken Sande, *The Peace Maker*, 215.

forgiveness and justice coexist. Again, however, even this truth, which was highlighted earlier, becomes distorted and undermined when unconditional forgiveness is presented as biblical teaching. Nevertheless, when the truth around forgiveness is understood, it takes on an entirely new dimension, and as such, it is incumbent upon us to examine what it means to genuinely forgive.

To start with, however, it may be beneficial to consider again what forgiveness is *not*. David Augsburger, for example, writes: "Forgiveness is far rarer than one assumes at first thought. More often it is not forgiveness that occurs, but pious denial, memory fade, polite avoidance, or deliberate subterfuge."[100] It should also be stressed that forgiveness is *not* a feeling, but rather, a commitment. Again, forgiveness is *not* forgetting, because forgetting is a passive process during which the matter fades from memory over time, and the more traumatic the event, the longer related memories take to fade. Again, in the context of the Northern Ireland conflict, where we are dealing with events as traumatic as the murder of a loved one, it must be recognised that those memories, quite often, will never really fade away.

In seeking to understand the commitment to forgive, therefore, we return to that key principle, which is that God expects Christians to forgive each other in exactly the same way that He forgave them. With this principle in mind, I refer again to Chris Brauns' definition when he writes: "God's forgiveness: A commitment by the one true God to pardon graciously those who repent and believe so they are reconciled to him, although this commitment does not eliminate all consequences."[101]

Again, I fully recognise that for many still hurting from the often-grievous wrongs committed against them, the thought of making such a commitment to forgive will seem nigh impossible. However, there are times when it is necessary again to focus on that bigger picture and ultimately consider what God may be teaching us in such circumstances. As stated earlier in this chapter, forgiveness, both in attitude and action,

[100]David Augsburger, The Freedom of Forgiveness, 53.
[101]Chris Brauns, *Unpacking Forgiveness* (Crossway, Wheaton, Illinois, 2008), 51.

requires extraordinary strength and commitment, the like of which is only available from a source outside of ourselves. Ken Sande doesn't beat about the bush when he presents the stark reality:

> "It is impossible to truly forgive others in your own strength, especially when they have hurt you deeply or betrayed your trust. You can try not to think about what they did or stuff your feelings deep inside and put on a false smile when you see them. But unless your heart is cleansed and changed by God, the memories and the feelings will still be lurking in the background, poisoning your thoughts and words, and preventing the rebuilding of trust and relationships."

> "There is only one way to remove these barriers," Sande concludes, and that is "to admit that you cannot forgive in your own strength and that you desperately need God to come in and change your heart."[102]

Jesus spoke into just such a situation where human strength is insufficient when He declared, *"With men this is impossible, but with God all things are possible."* (Matthew 19:26) Jesus, therefore, is not oblivious to the complexities surrounding forgiveness, particularly in challenging circumstances, hence the clear instruction in Luke 17:3 as regards the need for repentance. Using this passage as a starting point, Ken Sande reminds us that although "ideally, repentance should precede forgiveness," he draws the distinction between those "minor offences" that may be "overlooked and put away even if the offender has not expressly repented" and those offences "too serious to be overlooked and of which the offender has not yet repented."[103]

As regards those more serious offences, Ken Sande recommends a two-stage process. First, Sande recommends a correct "attitude" of forgiveness, i.e., "a loving and merciful attitude towards someone who has offended you. [Such an attitude Sande elaborates] will protect you

---

[102]Ken Sande, *The Peace Maker*, 205.
[103]Ibid., 210.

from bitterness and resentment."[104] Secondly, the actual granting of forgiveness, which again, although conditional for those more serious offences, is nonetheless a command when those conditions are met, thus "closing the matter forever."[105] It is imperative therefore that we remain focused on the bigger picture in regard to the fruits of forgiveness, namely that of achieving reconciliation, which restores harmony for ourselves, our families, and the wider society.

As has been alluded to previously, it is often the case that forgiveness is withheld or hindered by unrealistic, or even sinful expectations. Many, for example, may wilfully withhold forgiveness because they conclude that the offender does not deserve to be forgiven or because they still wish to somehow punish the offender for the suffering they have caused. Again, Ken Sande points out that, "these attitudes and expectations are utterly inconsistent with the command to forgive as God forgives us."[106]

Finally, Sande offers his definition of what should constitute forgiveness by way of four promises we should make when we truly forgive someone:

- I will not dwell on this incident
- I will not bring up this incident again and use it against
- I will not talk to others about this incident
- I will not let this incident stand between us or hinder our personal relationship[107]

Offering Forgiveness.

There is, however, one important misconception that must be addressed as regards the nature of genuine forgiveness, and that has come to manifest itself in a kind of "halfway house" position. This erroneous interpretation promotes the view that Christians must

---

[104]Ibid., 211.
[105]Ibid., 211.
[106]Ibid., 215.
[107]Ibid., 209.

unconditionally "offer" forgiveness, whereupon the onus then lies with the one being forgiven to accept that offer by way of repentance.

When we consider that genuine forgiveness is presented as an act that, when performed, closes the matter between the offender and the offended party once and for all, we can only conclude that the mere "offering" of forgiveness prior to confession and repentance, falls far short of such a position where closure is little more than a distant dream. While again, it is true that the Christian attitude towards an offender should be one of a *willingness to forgive,* with a view to being reconciled, it must be stressed that this willingness to forgive when the correct circumstances are met is not the same as offering forgiveness unconditionally, particularly in situations where little or no interaction has taken place between the opposing parties.

Lord Robin Eames, former Archbishop of Armagh and Church of Ireland Primate of All Ireland, in appearing to condone the practice of offering or "expressing" forgiveness, nonetheless acknowledges the shortcomings within this teaching. In his 2017 book "Unfinished Search," he writes, "While the individual action of expressing forgiveness to another human being produces a new relationship, it is questionable whether a person's acceptance of forgiveness expressed to them is essential for what can be termed a process to be successful."[108] The glaring problem that Lord Eames highlights is the impersonal nature of such a process, where no interaction has taken place, let alone any remorse having been expressed for the crimes committed. Referencing a bereaved mother, Lord Eames asks the pertinent question, "How could she forgive those she did not know? How could she tell them of her willingness to somehow come to her own terms of meeting what we so often call 'closure' when she could not speak directly to them?"[109]

The teaching that forgiveness must be "unconditionally offered" also leads to all manner of difficulty, particularly as regards "corporate

---

[108]Robin Eames, *Unfinished Search* (Columba Press, Dublin, 2017), 194.
[109]Ibid., 194.

forgiveness." If we accept the view that forgiveness can be offered unconditionally, there remains no barrier to the equally erroneous view that forgiveness can be offered to a corporate body. Jay Adams observes that the Bible says nothing about forgiving "masses of people whom we are unable to rebuke, whose confession of sin we could never hear."[110] Such a scenario therefore is clearly unworkable, again because of the personal nature of guilt and the inability to ascertain the genuineness of any subsequent repentance, not to mention the fact that many within the group supposedly being forgiven may be totally oblivious to what is actually taking place.

Before leaving this point, however, it is worth pointing out by way of clarification, that the Scriptures do make provision for a corporate body to administer forgiveness to an individual. Quoting Jay Adams again: "While forgiveness is primarily an individual matter, the Bible does recognise corporate forgiveness. This is forgiveness by *the church as a whole, as an organised body of believers*".[111] The power to exercise corporate forgiveness was given to the church by the Lord Jesus Himself, as recorded in John 20:23, *"If you forgive the sins of any, they are forgiven them; if you retain the sins of any, they are retained."* As previously examined, Jesus presented a model for administering church discipline as recorded in Matthew 18:15-17, and we find an example of corporate forgiveness being granted to a repentant church member in 2 Corinthians 2:5-11.

Genuine forgiveness, therefore, is a challenging subject, and as we will see in the following Bible accounts, the subject of forgiveness, as taught by Jesus, also caused the apostles, and many of his hearers, great difficulty. Much like today, Jesus was stepping into an environment that, as we have already experienced, was openly hostile to much of His teaching on the subject.

---

[110]Jay E. Adams, *From Forgiven to Forgiving* (Calvary Press, Amityville, NY, 1994), 29.
[111]Ibid., 114.

Chapter Eleven

Seventy Times Seven

Immediately after Jesus had issued the guidelines concerning forgiveness and reconciliation in the context of church discipline (which we addressed earlier), it is recorded that the apostle Peter, in seeking further clarification, asked the following question: *"Lord, how often shall my brother sin against me, and I forgive him? Up to seven times?"* (Matthew 18:21). Peter probably thought he was being rather magnanimous by suggesting one should forgive an offender "seven times," because up to that time it had been Jewish tradition that an offence need only be forgiven three times. This Jewish interpretation had been based on examples found in the first chapter of the book of Amos, where on several occasions, God pronounces that he will forgive a nation three times for their transgressions against Israel but will judge them accordingly on the fourth. However, Jesus again challenges the accepted order, and begins to emphasise the significance of forgiveness when He replies, *"I do not say to you, up to seven times, but up to seventy times seven"* (Matthew 18:22).

While the mathematician might quickly determine that Jesus is suggesting an offender should be forgiven 490 times, such number counting is to miss the point entirely. The radical message Jesus is relaying here is that forgiveness has nothing to do with scorekeeping, but rather that when an offender truly repents, forgiveness cannot be withheld. Confirmation of this stance is found when we delve a little further into another previously quoted passage. In Luke 17:3, we read: *"If your brother sins against you, rebuke him; and if he repents, forgive him."* However, the next verse reads; *"And if he sins against you seven times in a day, and seven times in a day returns to you, saying, 'I repent,' you shall forgive him"* (Luke 17:4).

While someone might ask what type of individual would sin against someone seven times in one day, and still have the gall to ask for forgiveness seven times; this is to miss the point. When we consider that we are to "forgive as God forgives," it is prudent in this context to remember that this is exactly how God forgives the Christian who remorsefully repents of numerous sins committed throughout each day, only to be forgiven by a merciful God. Likewise, the lesson in view here is that it cannot be justified to withhold forgiveness when a repentant offender seeks such forgiveness. John MacArthur concludes: "Jesus is teaching here that the forgiveness we extend to others should be as boundless as the mercy of God we desire for ourselves."[112]

At this point, many can become discouraged, and start to seek excuses. Not surprisingly, this was exactly the reaction of the apostles. Having heard Jesus' instruction that an offender must be forgiven, if need be, up to "seven times in a day," the apostles responded with the plea that they did not have enough faith to be able to comply with such a demand (Luke 17:5). However, Jesus was quick to counter this excuse and said, *"If you have faith as a mustard seed, you can say to this mulberry tree, 'Be pulled up by the roots and be planted in the sea,' and it would obey you."* In effect, Jesus was saying it was not a matter of faith, but of obedience. And by way of emphasising the point yet further, Jesus relays the duties of a hard-working servant, who, despite his arduous schedule, is still expected to fulfil *all* the duties expected of him (Luke 17:7-10).

The Unforgiving Servant

Returning to Matthew chapter 18, and following directly on from Jesus' reply to Peter's question: "Lord, how often shall my brother sin

---

[112]John MacArthur, *The Freedom and Power of Forgiveness*, 102.

against me, and I forgive him?" Jesus, by way of re-emphasising the point that when repentance is forthcoming there is no justification for withholding forgiveness, presents the following parable as recorded in Matthew 18:23-35:

> *"Therefore the kingdom of heaven is like a certain king who wanted to settle accounts with his servants. And when he had begun to settle accounts, one was brought to him who owed him ten thousand talents. But as he was not able to pay, his master commanded that he be sold, with his wife and children and all that he had, and that payment be made. The servant therefore fell down before him, saying, 'Master, have patience with me, and I will pay you all.' Then the master of that servant was moved with compassion, released him, and forgave him the debt. But that servant went out and found one of his fellow servants who owed him a hundred denarii; and he laid hands on him and took him by the throat, saying, 'Pay me what you owe!' So his fellow servant fell down at his feet and begged him, saying, 'Have patience with me, and I will pay you all.' And he would not, but went and threw him into prison till he should pay the debt. So when his fellow servants saw what had been done, they were very grieved, and came and told their master all that had been done. Then his master, after he had called him, said to him, 'You wicked servant! I forgave you all that debt because you begged me. Should you not also have had compassion on your fellow servant, just as I had pity on you?' And his master was angry, and delivered him to the torturers until he should pay all that was due to him. So My heavenly Father also will do to you if each of you, from his heart, does not forgive his brother his trespasses."*

Before attempting to glean the meaning of this parable, it is worth noting the comments of Jay Adams when he writes, "The parables, moreover, are not allegories in which every feature is paralleled with some point that is being made. Some of the details, therefore, are there simply to make the parable hold together as a story and serve no other function."[113] The primary aspect of this story therefore is clearly the rank hypocrisy of the first servant, who was mercifully forgiven much but who, in turn, refused to display any mercy and refused to forgive much less of his own servant. However, to glean the full significance of the parable, it is necessary to delve a little further.

The "King" in the story, represents God. While settling His accounts, a servant is brought before him who owes a great debt of "ten thousand talents." When we consider that one talent was the equivalent of 6000 denarii, and when we further consider that just one denarii was considered a fair day's wage (Matthew 20:2), we see that only one talent (6000 denarii) is the equivalent of seventeen years wages for the average worker. In effect, Jesus is relaying the fact that the servant's debt was simply beyond his means to pay. Following the servant's repentance and pleas for mercy, however (v 26), we see a picture of a compassionate King, who graciously forgives the debt and, in effect, suffers the loss himself.

Incidentally, it is the repentance and heartfelt pleas of the penitent servant that appear to have been overlooked by Timothy Keller as he portrays the King forgiving unconditionally, even going so far as to suggest that the relationship between this first servant and the King "breaks down" because the servant failed to repent *after* he had been forgiven.[114] Such a scenario, whereby God initially forgives the sinner in the hope that repentance will be forthcoming later, seems contrary to the plan for salvation plainly set forth through the teaching of Jesus and the writings of the apostles, where repentance is unequivocally presented as a prerequisite to the sinner's forgiveness.

As the story unfolds, however, we observe that the forgiven servant, upon leaving the presence of the King, encounters one of his own servants who owes him a relatively small amount of just one hundred denarii. The first servant unashamedly demands full and immediate restitution of the debt, and when his helpless fellow servant asks for

---

[113]Jay Adams, *From Forgiven to Forgiving*, 45.
[114]Timothy Keller *Forgive Why Should I And How Can I?*, 9.

time to pay, his master displays no mercy whatsoever and has his debtor cast into prison. News of this incident soon reaches the King, who has the wicked servant brought before him again, whereupon he is rightly castigated for his unforgiving spirit and cast into prison.

Before drawing any conclusions, it is helpful to remember the context in which Jesus is giving this lesson. The parable is primarily for the benefit of Peter and the apostles and, by implication, for Christian believers. The hypocritical servant represents a child of God, who, although having been forgiven the debt that none of us could ever hope to repay, fails to fully appreciate the mercy shown by his King and, as such, fails miserably to display that same forgiving spirit in his everyday life.

The discipline administered by way of the unforgiving servant being delivered "to the torturers," is *not*, as some suppose, a reference to eternal punishment in hell. Rather, the picture perfectly parallels the scenario already covered in relation to the petition from the Lord's prayer, "Forgive us our debts," where it was shown that the Children of God will find themselves being disciplined by a loving "Father," particularly if they display an unforgiving spirit towards others. Again, I reference Ken Sande's comment, which was written specifically concerning this passage: "Until we repent of this sinful attitude, we will suffer unpleasant circumstances. To begin with, we will feel separated from God and other Christians. We may also experience unusual hardships and lose blessings that would otherwise be ours."[115] John MacArthur draws a similar conclusion in regard to the closing scene from this parable:

> ".... The punishment administered, though extremely severe, seems to picture only the harshest kind of discipline, *not* eternal condemnation. The King "handed him [the wicked servant] over to the torturers," *not* the executioners, "until he should repay all that was owed" (v 34).

---

[115]Ken Sande, *The Peace Maker*, 217.

"Look at the verse closely," MacArthur continues: "What was *now* owed to the King? Since the earlier debt was already legally forgiven, the remaining debt was primarily this man's duty to show the same kind of mercy to others. The "torturers" represent the rod of God's discipline. The lesson of the parable is this. Christians who refuse to forgive others will be subject to the severest kind of discipline until they learn to forgive as they have been forgiven."[116]

The point of the entire parable, therefore, is to highlight yet again the sinful hypocrisy of the first servant, representing a child of God, who was mercifully forgiven much but who in turn only epitomised the nature of an unforgiving spirit by failing to display similar mercy towards others in that he refused to forgive his fellow servant.

---

[116]John MacArthur, The Freedom and Power of Forgiveness, 111.

Chapter Twelve

Forgiveness Takes Priority

Having learned that forgiveness is in effect non-negotiable when the respective circumstances are met, it is necessary to realise that forgiveness and the healing of relationships, particularly among believers, should take priority over everything else. This, of course, should not be a surprise, particularly when we consider how a damaged relationship might affect every aspect of our lives. It is, however, another example in relation to the worship life of the believer, which Jesus uses to bring home the urgency to seek reconciliation. Reading in Matthew 5:23-24; *"Therefore if you bring your gift to the altar, and there remember that your brother has something against you, leave your gift there before the altar, and go your way. First be reconciled to your brother, and then come and offer your gift."* Ken Sande comments on this passage:

> "If you learn that someone has something against you, God wants you to take the initiative in seeking peace – even if you do not believe you have done anything wrong. If you believe that the other person's complaints are unfounded or that the misunderstanding is entirely the other person's fault, you may naturally conclude that you have no responsibility to take the initiative in restoring peace. This is a common conclusion, but it is false."[117]

The lesson Jesus is presenting here is simply that if there is an ongoing dispute between yourself and someone else, regardless of whether you

---

[117]Ken Sande, The Peace Maker, 148

consider yourself at fault or not, then every effort must be made to sort the matter out as soon as possible. There are several reasons why someone should take the necessary steps to achieve reconciliation, regardless of who is at fault. Again, within the confines of the faith community, any sign of disharmony among believers will adversely affect how others might perceive the gospel. Commenting on this passage, John MacArthur states:

> "In any case, reconciliation is essential. If you have committed the offence, it is sinful not to make it right. If you are the offended party, you also have a duty to seek reconciliation – to try to win your brother. There is never any excuse for a Christian on either side of a broken relationship to refuse to pursue reconciliation."[118]

It should also be borne in mind that it is not uncommon for someone to be oblivious to the fact that they may have inadvertently offended another. Talking the matter over is the only way to ascertain the root of the problem before relationships come under more strain. Finally, the motivation must always be the love for a brother and the heartfelt desire that harmony would be restored, not only between believers but, more importantly, that the close relationship with God, exemplified by bringing "your gift to the alter," would be restored as well.

One final passage that also speaks to this specific situation is found in Mark 11:25-26. In relaying the benefits of faithful prayer (v 24), Jesus proceeds to highlight that one issue which will stifle the believer's interactions with God, when He states: *"And whenever you stand praying, if you have anything against anyone, forgive him, that your Father in heaven may also forgive you your trespasses. But if you do not forgive, neither will your Father in heaven forgive your trespasses."*

Again, this teaching aligns perfectly with the lesson we have already learned from our examination of the Lord's Prayer, primarily the phrase "forgive us our debts as we forgive our debtors," and the parable of the Unforgiving Servant. In both instances, it was explained that

---

[118]John MacArthur, The Freedom and Power of Forgiveness, 132.

failure to forgive as God has forgiven, can lead to a temporal loss of fellowship with God the Father and, by implication, negatively affect every aspect of our spiritual lives. However, in light of the particular significance placed upon this passage by theologians like Timothy Keller, who presents it as a way of supporting unconditional forgiveness, it is necessary to delve a little deeper or see how this passage sits within the wider teaching regarding biblical forgiveness.

To this end, John MacArthur highlights an important aspect in relation to this passage before us. He points out that the act of forgiveness called for here in Mark 11:25 is to be instantaneous and, as such, is to be granted even though no formal meeting or transaction has taken place. MacArthur concludes that the forgiveness referred to in Mark 11:25, is very different from the forgiveness of Luke 17:3.[119] Therefore, in proceeding, it is vital to examine the distinction between these two acts of forgiveness, and ask the question, is it necessary to "go and tell" a brother about every offence with a view to seeking recompense by way of repentance?

Common sense alone tells us that the answer is; "No." A scenario where repentance is sought for those many petty shortcomings that beset us all, would of course be totally unworkable, not to mention destructive to relationships. Can you even begin to imagine a marriage where the respective spouses were to keep account of all infringements with a view to thrashing out each and every minor issue? Although, to be fair, my list of minor infringements pertaining to my dear wife would be relatively small, while on the other hand, I would have to reluctantly admit that my wife's list of infringements against her spouse would, with some justification, be considerably longer. Or again, can you imagine the mayhem that would ensue within a church environment if parishioners were to seek redress for even minor offences caused either to themselves or to others?

Having got the picture, and in an attempt to bring some clarity, let us go back to the principles of church discipline as recorded in

---

[119]Ibid., 121.

Matthew 18:15-17, and specifically, the need for church discipline in the first instance. The reason for the four-stage process, starting with a one-to-one meeting between the offended party and the offender, and concluding with either reconciliation having been achieved or the offender being expelled from church membership was, as stated before, in order to maintain harmonious relationships and, by implication, protecting the integrity and purity of the *body* as a whole.

For example, the integrity and purity of the body will *not* be adversely affected by the actions of a young recently qualified driver, who upon driving to church for the first time, parks in the first space he sees, unwittingly blocking disabled access. Nor will the integrity and purity of the body be adversely affected when someone inadvertently places someone else's prized Bible in front of the video projector, resulting in a rather singed Bible being sheepishly returned to its owner shortly afterwards (and yes, I can bear witness to both incidents).

While it helped that restitution was offered for the aforementioned Bible, the fact remains that when it comes to those all-too-common small infringements, where more often than not, the offender may be oblivious to the fact that offence has been caused in the first place, the matter is best dealt with by a sprinkling of love, and moving on. It is also true, of course, that these practical and sensible principles pertaining to the overlooking of relatively minor matters should likewise be a guide as regards maintaining harmonious relationships in every aspect of our lives, both within the church environment and equally, within the wider community. Several Bible passages provide food for thought:

- o Proverbs 17:9: *"He who covers a transgression seeks love, But he who repeats a matter separates friends."*

- o 1 Corinthians 13:7: *"[Love] bears all things, believes all things, hopes all things, endures all things."*

- o Ephesians 4:2: *"with all lowliness and gentleness, with long-suffering, bearing with one another in love"*

○ 1 Peter 4:8: *"And above all things have fervent love for one another, for love will cover a multitude of sins."*

Referencing some of the above passages, Ken Sande writes:

> "In many instances, the best way to resolve a conflict is simply to overlook the personal offences of others. This approach is highly recommended throughout scripture – When we overlook the wrongs of others, we are imitating God's extraordinary forgiveness towards us. *"The Lord is compassionate and gracious, slow to anger, abounding in love. He will not always accuse, nor will he harbour his anger forever; he does not treat us as our sins deserve or repay us according to our iniquities"* (Psalm 103:8-10)."[120]

With these thoughts in mind, it is necessary to look again at a few passages that were previously examined earlier, namely Ephesians 4:31-32, Colossians 3:12-13, and Matthew 6:12. These passages were examined with a view to highlighting the fact that, as we are instructed to forgive *as* God forgives, they did not contradict the teaching that forgiveness per se is conditional upon repentance for more serious offences. However, as acknowledged at the time, there is a much broader application that calls for further explanation.

Ephesians 4:31-32 therefore, reads: *"Let all bitterness, wrath, anger, clamor, and evil speaking be put away from you, with all malice. And be kind to one another, tenderhearted, forgiving one another, just as God in Christ forgave you."* A similar sentiment is expressed in Colossians 3:12-13: *"Therefore, as the elect of God, holy and beloved, put on tender mercies, kindness, humility, meekness, long-suffering; bearing with one another, and forgiving one another, if anyone has a complaint against another; even as Christ forgave you, so you also must do."* Finally, we read again the relevant extract from the Lord's Prayer in Matthew 6:12, *"And forgive us our debts, as we forgive our debtors."*

---

[120]Ken Sande, *The Peace Maker*, 82.

Again, the clear emphases in the first two passages are very much on the forgiver, and in particular, the role forgiveness plays in maintaining good relationships marked by *kindness, humility, meekness,* and *long-suffering,* as opposed to contentious relationships marked with *bitterness, anger,* and *evil speaking.* And when these sentiments are considered again in light of the petition believers are called to pray: "Forgive us our debts, as we forgive our debtors," it is clear that the emphases are equally, if not in fact more so, on those minor, petty offences, which if not covered in love, have the potential to do real harm. It is not an overstatement therefore to say that when we are instructed in scripture to "forgive one another," that the emphasis is very much on reducing confrontation by way of encouraging a spirit of patience, benevolence, kindness, and mercy.

Returning to Mark 11:25, which reads: *"And whenever you stand praying, if you have anything against anyone, forgive him, that your Father in heaven may also forgive you your trespasses,"* again, the act of forgiveness sought here was to be instantaneous and granted without any interaction with the offender. As such, the passage clearly relates to some minor offence that the believer is to "cover in love." The following verse: *"But if you do not forgive, neither will your Father in heaven forgive your trespasses"* (v 26), as has already been pointed out, aligns the teaching perfectly with the lesson we have already learned from our examination of the Lord's Prayer, (*forgive us our debts as we forgive our debtors*), and the parable of the Unforgiving Servant, where the sin of an unforgiving heart is roundly condemned. To suggest that this example of forgiveness in Mark 11 should definitively shape our understanding of forgiveness per se, would effectively result in anarchy. As we will see when we come to look at another passage favoured by those who promote unconditional forgiveness, namely Jesus' command to *"turn the other cheek,"* it is important that the context and associated practical implications, must always be borne in mind.

Nevertheless, it is imperative that the Christian guard against the sin of hardheartedness, where a failure to deal with this *soul* problem can lead to all kinds of difficulties for the individual concerned by way of soured relationships, not least the believer's relationship with God. John MacArthur summarises: "Whenever possible, especially if the offence is petty or unintentional, it is best to forgive unilaterally. This is the very essence of a gracious spirit. It is the Christlike attitude called for in Ephesians 4:1-3:

> *"I, therefore, the prisoner of the Lord, beseech you to walk worthy of the calling with which you were called, with all lowliness and gentleness, with long-suffering, bearing with one another in love, endeavoring to keep the unity of the Spirit in the bond of peace."*[121]

Turn the Other Cheek

Another oft quoted phrase attributed to Jesus, which is frequently misused when taken out of context, is found in Matthew 5:39, where we read: *"But I tell you not to resist an evil person. But whoever slaps you on your right cheek, turn the other to him also."* First of all, it must be pointed out that it would make no sense to interpret the passage to imply that Jesus is saying that we are to permit the "evil person" to do whatever he pleases. Clearly, such a view would contradict the plain teaching of scripture in that, *"the face of the Lord is against those who do evil"* (1 Peter 3:12). Believers themselves are called to, *"Resist the devil"* (James 4:7), and *"wrestle against...evil"* (Ephesians 6:12), to give just three examples. Commenting on Matthew 5:39, Ken Sande brings clarity and offers good advice:

> "This passage does not forbid personal correction. Rather, it forbids people to take the law into their own hands and seek vengeance against those who wrong them. This verse teaches that Christians should be willing to endure personal injury without retaliation when that injury comes as a direct result of their Christian witness."[122]

---

[121]John MacArthur, *The Freedom and Power of Forgiveness*, 123.
[122]Ken Sande, The Peace Maker, 153.

Here Jesus warns us to guard against the temptation to retaliate or seek revenge; to resist the all too easily made spiteful comment in response to provocation from someone with evil intent. In fact, when the entire passage is taken in context (verses 39–48) Jesus is outlining the basic Christian principle that believers are to *"do good to those who hate you"* (v 44). While this vital principle will be examined to a fuller extent later in the study, concentrating again on verse 39, and the phrase *"But whoever slaps you on your right cheek, turn the other to him also,"* John MacArthur concludes:

> "Christ was not teaching that evil agents should simply be allowed to have their way in all circumstances. Jesus Himself opposed evil doers constantly, through His teaching and His actions. On two occasions He even made a whip of cords and drove out those who were profaning His Father's house (Matthew 21:12; John 2:15)."[123]

As we have ascertained in Matthew 18:15-17, unrepentant evil-doers within the church were to be opposed and barred from church membership. And of course, the "turn the other cheek" principle cannot be meant to keep civil government from punishing evildoers. To apply these principles in the civil arena would, according to MacArthur, "surrender society to chaos."[124] In closing this section, I can only add that such a scenario would, of course, also contradict clear biblical teaching, which states that God-ordained civil governments are to be "a terror to" those who do "evil" (Romans 13:3).

---

[123]John MacArthur, The Freedom and Power of Forgiveness, 35.
[124]Ibid., 35.

Chapter Thirteen

Removing the Plank

There is one final, but nonetheless vital, point to remember before we seek to point a finger and accuse another of sin. All too often, an unforeseen barrier exists when it comes to travelling the road to forgiveness and meaningful reconciliation, particularly when relationships appear to have broken down. When one party is so convinced they are blameless, it is all too easy to judge the other party accordingly. The Lord Jesus Himself speaks directly into just such a situation, and presents this clear admonishment recorded for us in Matthew 7:1-5:

> *"Judge not, that you be not judged. For with what judgment you judge, you will be judged; and with the measure you use, it will be measured back to you. And why do you look at the speck in your brother's eye, but do not consider the plank in your own eye? Or how can you say to your brother, 'Let me remove the speck from your eye'; and look, a plank is in your own eye? Hypocrite!* **First** *remove the plank from your own eye, and then you will see clearly to remove the speck from your brother's eye."*

Jesus is warning his listeners here that there is something which must be attended to *first*, before you enter into judgement against another. However, before we proceed, it is also worth pointing out that the opening phrase, "Judge not, that you be not judged," does not, as is often claimed, forbid *judging* per se, not least because believers are instructed in Matthew 7:15-20 that "false prophets" or false teachers, would be identifiably by their "fruits" or works. Clearly, therefore, the identification of these imposters was to be dependent upon the believer exercising due diligence and "judging" the *works* of such teachers to determine their authenticity.

Returning to the overall theme of Matthew 7:1-5, it is clear that Jesus is addressing the humility and honesty by which the *judging* was to be conducted. Commenting on this passage, Matthew Henry issues a warning when he writes, "Pride and uncharitableness are commonly beams in the eyes of those that pretend to be critical and nice in their censures of others."[125] Self-righteous pride, and an uncharitable nature, are two attributes which must be strongly guarded against when it comes to resolving disputes and building reconciliation. We do well, therefore, to remember again that, "*all have sinned and fall short of the glory of God*" (Romans 3:23).

Commenting on this passage, Ken Sande also points out that, "it forbids *premature and improper* correction. Before you talk to others about their faults, Jesus warns you to face up to yours."[126] And referring back to chapter four of this book, titled, "We Never Walk Alone," it is also necessary to remind ourselves of those prejudices that will all too easily cloud our judgement when assessing the offences or shortcomings of others. David Augsburger presents a stark assessment regarding this destructive characteristic:

> "Prejudice is not simply a poor social judgement, a personal foible, or an excusable bias that is a quaint quirk of some persons or personalities. It is a serious mental illness. It can be diagnosed, defined, and named as a mental disorder which judges, alienates, devalues, distances, denigrates, and ultimately destroys humanness and human community.

---

[125]Matthew Henry Commentary, https://www.biblestudytools.com/commentaries/matthew-henry-complete/matthew/7.html - Accessed 01/03/2022
[126]Ken Sande, The Peace Maker, 79.

Prejudices, like all other mental illness has components that are learned from the values of the family and community, where one is taught the contents and objects of prejudice.

You and I are infected. We are all prejudiced. What's more, we are carriers. Our children catch it from us as they "catch on" to the hidden meanings of our uncaring words or unfeeling jokes. Any slip of the tongue, innocent as it may seem, transmits the fetid contents of a disease spot festering in the dark recesses of the unconscious."[127]

Scripture, of course, warns us that the tongue is often a chief cause of conflict. James 3:5-8 reads: "*Even so the tongue is a little member and boasts great things. See how great a forest a little fire kindles! And the tongue is a fire, a world of iniquity. The tongue is so set among our members that it defiles the whole body, and sets on fire the course of nature… no man can tame the tongue. It is an unruly evil, full of deadly poison.*"

While reckless words, spoken in haste, will indeed inflame conflict, it is also the case that the tongue of the wise can bring healing. Consider Proverbs 12:18: "*There is one who speaks like the piercings of a sword, But the tongue of the wise promotes health.*" Speaking of the tongue, Ken Sande presents such wisdom when he writes, "…make every effort to breathe grace by saying only what is both true and helpful, speaking well of your opponent whenever possible, and using kind and gracious language."[128]

Sande summarises the matter succinctly: "When you follow Jesus' teaching, your confession will sometimes encourage the other person to admit sins."[129] Whereas on the other hand, an angry self-righteous comment can do great harm, just as the writer of Proverbs declares: "*A brother offended is harder to win than a strong city, And contentions are like the bars of a castle*" (Proverbs 18:19). Failure, therefore, to acknowledge the "plank" in our own eye, will diminish our ability to clearly see the path ahead, particularly a path that could lead to reconciliation.

---

[127]David Augsburger, *The New Freedom of Forgiveness*, 99-100
[128]Ken Sande, *The Peace Maker*, 249.
[129]Ken Sande, *The Peace Maker*, 158.

R.T. Kendall also writes concerning this aspect: "When we are indignant over someone's wickedness, there is a real possibility that either we are self-righteous or that we have no objectivity about ourselves." Kendal continues, "When we see ourselves as we are, we will see that we may well be capable of any sin ever committed by anyone save by God's intervening grace."[130] Speaking personally, I know myself only too well to recognise the uncomfortable truth contained within this statement. As someone who was far from immune to the emotions ignited by way of the conflict in Northern Ireland, to which I will testify later, I am already condemned a murderer in God's eyes because Scripture declares: *"Whoever hates his brother is a murderer, and you know that no murderer has eternal life abiding in him"* (1 John 3:15).

An honest recognition of our standing, therefore, before a Holy God, will help us guard against self-righteousness. Quoting James 2:10: *"For whoever shall keep the whole law, and yet stumble in one point, he is guilty of all,"* Ken Sande states: "Turning to the Bible and reminding yourselves of God's holiness will help you see more clearly the seriousness of even your smallest sin."[131] Keeping these truths in mind will help guard against the worthy cause of confronting an offender being undermined by a self-righteous and even prideful spirit. As regards the correct attitude when dealing with disputes, the apostle Paul gives commendable advice to the young Timothy when he writes, *"a servant of the Lord must not quarrel but be gentle to all… in humility correcting those who are in opposition, if God perhaps will grant them repentance, so that they may know the truth"* (2 Timothy 2:24-25).

Of course, there is no better example of humility in times of suffering than that displayed by Christ Himself. The apostle Peter recounts the example set by Jesus *"who, when He was reviled, did not revile in return; when He suffered, He did not threaten, but committed Himself to Him who judges righteously"* (1 Peter 2:23-24). Commenting on this passage, John MacArthur concludes: "When we suffer wrongfully, it becomes very easy to rationalise a counterattack and painfully difficult

---

[130]R.T. Kendall, *Total Forgiveness* (Hodder & Stoughton Ltd, London, 2010), 56.
[131]Ken Sande, *The Peace Maker*, 217.

to follow our Lord's steps. But like Him, we must keep entrusting ourselves to the One who Judges righteously."[132]

When Repentance is Necessary

In Matthew 18:15-17, we considered the practical implications of church discipline, in that such discipline was necessary to maintain harmonious relationships, and by implication protecting the integrity and purity of the *Body*. When we come to ascertain what constitutes a more serious offence in the civil arena, namely an offence which demands approaching an offender to "tell him his fault" with a view to seeking an admission of wrongdoing and repentance, I would propose that those basic principles which necessitate the need for church discipline, should broadly govern our attitude to ordinary everyday life as well. Basically, I would suggest that any offence which has the potential to shatter harmony or create discord within the family, or within the wider society or community, cannot simply be overlooked, but rather, must be openly addressed.

Before proceeding, however, it is perhaps necessary to point out that the phrase found in Matthew 18:15: *"if your brother sins against you,"* has a wider application than may first appear. While the King James and the New King James Bible versions render the passage: *"if your brother **sins against you,**"* some modern translations like the English Standard Version and the New American Standard Bible, reflect the fact that some ancient manuscripts simply render the phrase "if your brother sins." John MacArthur addresses this anomaly: "The textual variation turns out to be relatively unimportant... when we realise that all disciplinable sins are sins against the entire Body of Christ. So whether the other person's sin is *directly* "against thee" or only *indirectly...* go and show him his fault."[133]

It is not necessary, therefore, to be the actual injured party. Rather, there is still an obligation to approach the offender if, for example,

---

[132]John MacArthur, *The Freedom and Power of Forgiveness*, 51.
[133]Ibid., 144

you observe a brother in a morally compromising position, or perhaps you witness someone committing an offence which is likely to cause undue hurt or distress to another. Such offences, if not addressed, have the very real potential to disrupt the integrity of the church body, and in the contest of wider society, can also lead to disharmony. By way of substantiating this view, we observe the apostle Paul rebuking the Corinthian believers for tolerating such sins in *their* community (1 Corinthians 5), and elsewhere in scripture, believers are forbidden from overlooking wrongs committed against another:

- Exodus 23:6: "*You shall not pervert the judgment of your poor in his dispute.*"

- Deuteronomy 16:20: "*You shall follow what is altogether just, that you may live and inherit the land which the Lord your God is giving you.*"

- Isaiah 1:17: "*Learn to do good; Seek justice, Rebuke the oppressor; Defend the fatherless, Plead for the widow.*"

- Lamentations 3:35-36: "*to deny a man justice in the presence of the Most High, to subvert a man in his lawsuit, the Lord does not approve.*" (ESV)

As we seek now to apply these principles to wider society by way of administering justice and maintaining harmony, I would suggest that those more serious offences which cannot simply be overlooked broadly fall into the following categories:

- Physical injury, as a consequence of an angry or reckless act

- Deliberate theft of goods or property

- Wilful deception

- Malicious slandering of someone

- Crimes of immorality

Within the backdrop to our overall study therefore, namely that of terrorist violence associated with the Northern Ireland conflict, the evidence declares that many of those offences which were committed over the thirty years of that conflict, fall into all five of these categories. And again, in the context of this study, it must be borne in mind that not only do over 50% of the murders alone remain unsolved,[134] but it is also the case that the murderers themselves continue to be eulogised, with the result that effectual forgiveness which has the potential to produce meaningful reconciliation, remains afar off.

The basic premise that some sins are more serious than others, and therefore require decisive action, is shared by Ken Sande, who points out that God calls us to approach an offender "if that person's sins are too serious to overlook. This is why Jesus said, *"If your brother sins, rebuke him, and if he repents, forgive him"* (Luke 17:3).[135] Sande further references the following passages by way of substantiating that position.

- o Leviticus 19:17: *"You shall not hate your brother in your heart. You shall surely rebuke your neighbour, and not bear sin because of him."*

- o Proverbs 24:11: *"Deliver those who are drawn toward death, and hold back those stumbling to the slaughter."*

- o Proverbs 27:5-6: *"Open rebuke is better Than love carefully concealed. Faithful are the wounds of a friend, But the kisses of an enemy are deceitful."*

- o James 5:19-20: *"Brethren, if anyone among you wanders from the truth, and someone turns him back, let him know that he who turns a sinner from the error of his way will save a soul from death and cover a multitude of sins."*

Again, as we consider the civil environment and the basic enforcement of law and order, it is a well-established practice that while some offences will require little more than a cautionary warning, there are of

---

[134]Joint Authors (William Matchett) The *Northern Ireland Question Perspectives on Nationalism and Unionism* (Wordsworth Publishing 2020), 209.
[135]Ken Sande, The Peace Maker, 150.

course more serious offences which will require a police investigation, which in turn may lead to a court hearing and untimely to a sentence being enforced upon an offender. When we further consider that English common law, which operated successfully for centuries, was based on biblical principles, are we not perfectly entitled to ask, "how did the basic teaching around forgiveness and reconciliation become so complicated?"

To summarise, therefore: For those more serious offences, which fall into the categories referred to above, the believer is perfectly entitled to withhold forgiveness until there has been a recognition on the part of the offender that a wrong has been committed. Furthermore, it is advised that any subsequent act of repentance be measured against the practical guidelines previously presented under the heading "Genuine Repentance."

Alas however, having adopted this position in relation to repentance and forgiveness, I am only too well aware that there will be many who will seek to counter and say that such a model is unworkable, primarily because of the negative emotions such a course of action will inevitably store up. On the contrary, in the next chapter, I will examine the claims that are often levelled against those of us who argue that in extreme circumstances, forgiveness should *not* be granted unconditionally.

Chapter Fourteen

Unresolvable Conflict

We come now to arguably the most sensitive aspect of forgiveness, and to an area where a great deal of harm has been inflicted on victims and survivors, not to mention the damage done to the authority of Scripture, and by implication, the justice of God. Promoting the view that forgiveness must be unconditionally granted to an unrepentant offender, even for the most serious crimes, coupled with the erroneous teaching that failure to grant forgiveness in such circumstances, is a sin, has served only to re-traumatise many victims and survivors. When it is then further asserted that forgiving an offender is necessary from a therapeutic perspective, in order to elevate those negative emotions of bitterness and animosity, such ill-conceived advice has caused many to step back from their faith altogether, thus creating a barrier between themselves and those attempting to open up a discussion from a biblical perspective today. Time and time again, in order to gain a level of trust during my discussions with victims and survivors, both collectively and in private, it was necessary first of all to dispel the perception that I was simply another "religious do-gooder," coming to preach to them about how they must learn to forgive and move on.

That said, however, it must be acknowledged that where serious offences are not brought to a conclusion by way of repentance on the part of the offender, coupled with the fact that the victim may also have been denied justice, there is the very real possibility that the innocent party will succumb to negative feelings. Ken Sande writes:

"Unresolved conflict can lead to many types of "prisons" and can exact penalties we never anticipated. In addition to robbing you of time, property, or money, prolonged conflict can damage your relationships and destroy your reputation. It can imprison you in a dungeon of self-pity, resentment, or bitterness."[136]

In seeking to present his newly discovered "total forgiveness," as the solution to preventing the injured party from manifesting those undesirable feelings of "bitterness," R.T. Kendal writes: "Total forgiveness must take place in the heart for otherwise it is worthless. … If we have not truly forgiven, in our hearts, those who have hurt us, then it will come out – sooner or later." On the contrary, however, David Augsburger cautions against the view that this "inner forgiveness" such as that promoted by R.T. Kendal is a solution to these problems when he declares:

"When the forgiveness we understand is a *private process of inner healing, not* an interpersonal bridge that can stretch across the empty void between two injured persons to reconcile differences and restore relationships, it [too] feeds and fosters acts of resentment, revenge, retaliation, or demanding repayment."[137]

Continuing to reflect on the shortcomings of "inner forgiveness," Augsburger adds: "In the modern world, writing on forgiveness is almost exclusively focused on the process within, the virtues of the freedom found by the forgiver. It is common for teaching on forgiveness *never to get to what Jesus actually taught*, but to focus only on tolerance and love."[138]

And this brings me to my main contention with those who promote unconditional forgiveness, namely the erroneous view that the *only* way to alleviate those negative emotions of resentment and bitterness,

---

[136]Ken Sande, The Peace Maker, 90.
[137]David Augsburger, The New Freedom of Forgiveness, 20.
[138]Ibid., 25.

etc., is to forgive the offender unconditionally. For example, June Hunt writes: "When you refuse to forgive, your unforgiveness keeps you emotionally stuck to both the offence and the offender."[139] Steve Chalke is more forthright when he states: "We nod in agreement with the *experts* who tell us unforgiveness is a cancer that eats you from the inside and that *the act of forgiving* is healing and renewing."[140]

In this environment, therefore, the act of granting forgiveness is presented as the only way to counter such negative feelings, which over time have the very real potential to cause mental and even physical harm to the one who has been wronged. While I do not disagree that such negative feelings, if not addressed, can very often lead to mental and physical health issues, I would very much contend that the granting of *something dressed up as forgiveness*, which in effect is nothing like biblical forgiveness, serves anyone well in the long term. Such unconditional forgiveness, which is presented as little more than a feeling, fails every test when compared to biblical forgiveness, which demands a commitment to pardon an offender.

It should also be borne in mind that those who would argue for unconditional forgiveness by way of emphasising the psychological or therapeutic benefits for the one granting forgiveness, would do well to note that in those cases where the seriousness of the offence requires the offender to be challenged with a view to seeking reconciliation by way of repentance; the Bible always presents the actual granting of forgiving as something which happens between two parties. In concurring with an earlier quote from David Augsburger in relation to "unconditional inner forgiveness," Chris Brauns turns the table on those would promote such unconditional forgiveness when he states: "I believe that the notion of automatic forgiveness itself fosters bitterness. We are created with a standard of justice written on our hearts."[141]

---

[139]June Hunt, *Forgiveness The Freedom To Let Go* (Hendrickson Publishers, Massachusetts, USA, 2013), 26.
[140]Steve Chalke, *The Lost Message of Jesus*, 103.
[141]Chris Brauns *Unpacking Forgiveness* (Crossway, Wheaton, Illinois, 2008), 147.

A Time to Hate

It must first be recognised that victims, particularly of violent crime, will understandably go through a wide range of emotions. Even in the Old Testament book of Ecclesiastes, it is recorded that *"to everything there is a season, a time for every purpose under heaven.… a time to love, and **a time to hate**; a time of war, and a time of peace"* (Ecclesiastes 3:1 & 8). The author of Ecclesiastes is presenting the reality that during our lives on earth, there is a time for every activity and a time when we will experience every emotion.

Commenting on these contrasting emotions, Matthew Henry states that the time to love is a time; "to show ourselves friendly, to be free and cheerful, and it is a pleasant time; but [Matthew Henry continues] there may come a time to hate, when we shall see cause to break off all familiarity with some that we have been fond of, and to be upon the reserve, as having found reason for a suspicion, which love is loath to admit."[142] In this context, hate is presented as the opposite of love, and as with love, the term hate has a broad application. In Ecclesiastes 3:8, hatred is portrayed as an emotion which causes us to break relationship, and in effect places us in a position where we want nothing to do with the object of hate. This, I would suggest, is a perfectly natural emotion from time to time.

John Stott, when commenting on Jesus' command to *"love your enemies, bless those who curse you, do good to those who hate you"* (Matthew 5:44), proposes that those opposing emotions of love and hatred can even be in evidence at the same time. He writes:

> "The truth is that evil men should be the object simultaneously of our 'love' and of our 'hatred,' as they are simultaneously the objects of God's (although his 'hatred' is expressed as 'wrath'). To 'love' them is ardently to desire that they will repent and believe, and so be saved. To 'hate' them is to desire with equal ardour that,

---

[142]https://www.biblestudytools.com/commentaries/matthew-henry-complete/ecclesiastes/3.html - Accessed 08/02/2022

if they stubbornly refuse to repent and believe, they will incur God's judgement."

Stott concludes: "There is such a thing as perfect hatred, just as there is such a thing as righteous anger. But it is hatred for *God's* enemies, not our own enemies. It is entirely free of all spite, rancour and vindictiveness, and is fired only by love for God's honour and glory."[143]

As regards the volatile emotion of anger itself, in many Christian environments, believers have been conditioned to regard anger as something shameful. However, David Augsburger provides thoughtful insight when drawing the distinction between "destructive anger" and "constructive anger:"

> "Destructive anger drives people apart, severs relationships, settles into the floor of the soul [and] contaminates all other feelings, [while] Constructive anger seeks to break through the walls, yearns to remove barriers, presses to open communication, mobilizes energy to work at injustices and searches opportunities to reach out to the other in genuine contact."[144]

Augsburger goes on to describe different manifestations of constructive anger, including "creative anger" which he asserts can be "transformative, regenerative, and renewing in reforming a person" as they become empowered to shake off old resentments. Citing Gandhi and Martin Luther King Jr. as examples, such anger, continues Augsburger, "can be a great service to others," as injustices are challenged and wrongs are righted.[145]

Disciplined Anger can also be a positive emotion, argues Augsburger. "When we no longer feel deeply, care passionately, or speak forthrightly… about justice and what is right, when "anything goes," when everything is tolerated, all is lost."[146] All too often today, the

---

[143]John R.W. Stott, *The Message of The Sermon On The Mount* (Inter-Varsity Press, Leicester, England 1978) 117.
[144]David Augsburger, The New Freedom of Forgiveness, 60.
[145]Ibid., 63.
[146]Ibid., 63.

church cowers for fear of causing offence, and stands by as *evil is called good, and good evil"* (Isaiah 5:20). Within some compromising Christian environments, therefore, to display disciplined anger is labelled as being ungracious.

Finally, David Augsburger speaks of "purposeful anger" which he further defines as "effective anger, clarified anger, clearly articulated anger, distinctly moral anger. Creative and reconstructive anger is our hope, our power for change, our incentive to grow and our courage to act."[147] Jesus, who was "grieved by anger" against the rigid, unfeeling traditions of the Pharisees, deliberately antagonised them by healing the sick in front of their eyes on the Sabbath day (Mark 3:4-5). And that same anger was evidenced when Jesus whipped the "money changers" out of the Temple and into the street for daring to pollute God's holy sanctuary.

Anger in itself is therefore not a wholly destructive force; however, when it comes to "hatred," it must be stressed that the Bible is crystal clear in relation to the negative connotations that result from fostering or dwelling on hateful thoughts towards those whom we would regard as our enemies, which over time can develop into something more sinister. In Proverbs 10:12, we read: *"Hatred stirs up conflict, but love covers over all wrongs."* And the apostle Paul, writing to believers in Ephesus, declares, *"Get rid of all bitterness, rage and anger, brawling and slander, along with every form of malice"* (Ephesians 4:31). American Pastor Harry Emerson Fosdick, writing in the 1930s puts it succinctly, "Hating people is like burning down your own house to get rid of a rat."[148]

We must never underestimate the power and destructive nature of hatred. Those who harbour or promote hatred towards others, either deliberately or unwittingly, unleash a very destructive force. And it's that negative force that has wreaked so much pain and anguish in Ireland over the centuries, both among victims and perpetrators alike, and that continues to sour relationships today.

---

[147]Ibid., 64-65.
[148]Harry Emerson Fosdick, *As I See Religion*, (Harper & Brothers, New York, 1932)

In his book "The True Believer," in which American philosopher Eric Hoffer examines fanaticism, he perhaps sheds some light on why deep-seated hatred often characterises and sustains violent aggression by subversive groupings. Hoffer writes:

> "That hatred springs more from self-contempt than from a legitimate grievance is seen in the intimate connection between hatred and a guilty conscience. There is perhaps no surer way of infecting ourselves with virulent hatred towards a person than by doing him a grave injustice. That others have a just grievance against us is a more potent reason for hating them than that we have a just grievance against them." Hoffer concludes, "Self-righteousness is a loud din to drown the voice of guilt within us. There is a guilty conscience behind every brazen word and act and behind every manifestation of self-righteousness."[149]

Such a scenario would go some way to explaining the self-perpetuating animosities that kept the conflict going for over thirty years, and indeed, continue to provide the motivation to justify the violence of the past, lest the cries of resentment die down and the conscience is heard instead.

Courtesy is an Essential Quality

As alluded to earlier, I freely admit that, like so many involved in the conflict, I was certainly not immune to those same negative emotions. Having joined the police force at the all too tender age of eighteen, and while not oblivious to the sectarian tensions in the country, the open hostility I was to witness in my formative years of service in the late 1970s brought me into the real world of policing in Northern Ireland with quite a *bang...* literally. Within a matter of weeks of taking up my first posting, I experienced my first brush with death. A bomb, designed to murder police officers on a routine journey to

---

[149]Eric Hoffer, *The True Believer*, (Harper Collins Publishers, New York, 2019), 118.

relieve personnel at a permanent border checkpoint, was concealed in a vehicle parked on the route. Fortunately, on that occasion, the location of the bomb vehicle had raised suspicions, and having been redirected to clear the area as a safety precaution, the device was subsequently detonated by the IRA terrorists, who had been observing the scene from their trigger point across the border in the Irish Republic.

Further proof, if proof were needed, as to the level of determination to kill police officers came by way of an IRA gun attack on our vehicle just a month or so later. Again, providence was on our side, as after the initial shots, which suffice to say, alerted us to the attack, the assailant's weapon jammed, and he was forced to flee the scene without causing harm or injury. The upshot of those early traumatic experiences served only to convince me, rightly or wrongly, that there were people who really hated everything I stood for. I was perceived to be a representative of some "British occupation," and by implication a foreigner in the land where my ancestors had lived since before the founding of America. Looking back now, however, it is with a sense of much shame and regret that I admit my initial response was to hate them straight back! The murders and attempted murders of friends and colleagues over the following years, only served to add fuel to the fire.

The first definition of good policing is *courtesy*. The definition reads: "Courtesy is an essential quality and one which will smooth many a path. The public have a right to expect it, and with it, its complimentary quality, good manners." Suffice to say, as I look back now with a wiser head, there were many occasions when such courtesy on my part was sadly lacking; little knowing that I was merely "burning down my own house" to be rid of that elusive "rat." Again, with hindsight, I'm often haunted by the question, "Could a harsh word or action on my part have ever driven a young man into the arms of the Republican movement, thereby destroying his life, not to mention potentially the lives of many others?"

Chapter Fifteen

Do Not Repay Evil for Evil

"Hatred" is a dangerous and destructive emotion which, if not kept in check, will cause untold damage. First, when someone has been wronged in the manner of those more serious offences suggested earlier; i.e., a physical injury, theft of goods, wilful deception or slander, etc., it is important that we don't respond in kind. In Romans 12:17-21, the apostle Paul clearly details the Christian response when confronted with such circumstances:

> "Repay no one evil for evil. Have regard for good things in the sight of all men. If it is possible, as much as depends on you, live peaceably with all men. Beloved, do not avenge yourselves, but rather give place to wrath; for it is written, "Vengeance is Mine, I will repay," says the Lord. Therefore "If your enemy is hungry, feed him; If he is thirsty, give him a drink; For in so doing you will heap coals of fire on his head." Do not be overcome by evil, but overcome evil with good."

Paul here relays the two basic principles which must govern the Christian's response to a serious offence where no resolution seems possible. The most important principle is highlighted three times in the passage. In verse 17, we read, "Repay no one evil for evil"; in verse 19 we read again, "Beloved, do not avenge yourselves"; and in verse 21, "Do not be overcome by evil." All too often in our modern secular culture, through film and television, revenge is portrayed as the right and noble thing. The uncomfortable evidence from our conflict here in Northern Ireland, however, has only revealed that such actions serve little other than to exacerbate the problem, as the cycle of violence continues to grow.

David Augsburger, lays bare an uncomfortable truth as regards unresolved conflict resulting from those more serious offences, when he writes, "So few sins can be paid for, and so seldom does the victim possess the power or the advantage to demand payment." Acknowledging that "in most cases, making things right" is beyond possibility," Augsburger asks, "What then of revenge?" When restitution is impossible, it is all too easy to seek exact revenge on the offender. However, in reply to his own question, Augsburger cautions against such a course of action: "But here too, there is an intrinsic and insurmountable problem – as you try to get even, you actually become even with your enemy. You bring yourself to the same level, and below."[150]

Nora Bradford, wife of murdered MP Rev Robert Bradford, writing in her 2021 book titled, "When Time is Taken," poignantly summarises the conflicting emotions when she writes:

> "To have lost someone to terrorists and to think murderous thoughts, to want someone dead, or to want them to suffer excruciatingly as I have, is human and justifiable some would say. To do these things in my heart but to choose to repent is to find a better way through. To give myself over to a depraved mindset is to become as them. To stay bitter and steeped in anger, though totally justified, would allow me to become the very person that has brought sorrow, grief and horror to us and our land. I want a different heritage for my family."[151]

There is good reason, therefore, why the Bible condemns revenge. It serves no one well; neither the offender nor the victim, and only exacerbates many of the problems that brought about the initial conflict.

---

[150]David Augsburger, *The New Freedom of Forgiveness*, 18.
[151]Nora Bradford, When Time is Taken (Maurice Wylie Media, 2021), 188-189.

Returning to Romans chapter 12, a second guiding principle is revealed in verses 17b – 18, where we read: *"Have regard for good things in the sight of all men. If it is possible, as much as depends on you, live peaceably with all men,"* and again in verses 20, *"If your enemy is hungry, feed him; If he is thirsty, give him a drink; For in so doing you will heap coals of fire on his head."* While the first principle alone challenges our carnal tendencies, especially where a great deal of anger and resentment remain, this second principle takes us even further along a pathway which many will find uncomfortable to travel. However, the apostle Paul is not oblivious to these challenges and the limitations on what can be achieved, particularly when seeking to "live peaceably with all men," which invariably includes unbelievers.

We notice first, therefore, that the command is qualified by the use of the phrase, "If it is possible." Paul is well aware of the realities involved, and as such, our expectations at all times should be realistic. Jay Adams spells out the daily reality of dealing with unbelievers:

> "Unbelievers do not know the true God, they are self-centred rather than oriented towards God and others, do not possess the Holy Spirit, and so cannot love God or man in ways that are acceptable to God (Romans 8:5; 1 Corinthians 2). They cannot understand the Bible (1 Corinthians 2:6-16), and if they did, they wouldn't want to follow it, or couldn't. In short, as Paul put it, *"Those who are in the flesh [unbelievers] cannot please God"* (Romans 8:8)."[152]

Ken Sande also points out the limitations involved when dealing with difficult people. "Even when you continue to do what is right, some people may adamantly refuse to admit you are right or to live at peace with you." Sande advocates therefore that while the believer should still do all they can to be reconciled to others, they must accept that "you cannot force others to do what is right."[153]

---

[152]Jay E. Adams, *From Forgiven to Forgiving* (Calvary Press, Amityville, NY, 1994), 74.
[153]Ken Sande, The Peace Maker, 252.

However, returning to Romans 12:18, and paying particular attention to the phrase, *"as much as depends on you,"* it is clear that the onus is still very much on the believer as the one expected to take the initiative and act properly in such relationships. The believer is the one who must be seen to do as much as possible to preserve peace. This, of course, is not advocating that the believer is to be a "door mat;" rather, Paul is urging the believer to conduct themselves honourable in the presence of all men, with a view to establishing trust and stable relationships. To this end, Paul gives a further example when he states: *"Therefore "If your enemy is hungry, feed him; If he is thirsty, give him a drink; For in so doing you will heap coals of fire on his head"* (v 20). These challenging words by Paul, in effect, mirror those equally challenging words of Jesus as recorded in Matthew 5:44 where we read: *"But I say to you, love your enemies, bless those who curse you, do good to those who hate you."*

With a view to grasping exactly what Jesus and Paul are saying here, it is first necessary to understand what is meant by the term "love." In stating that the command is to love one's enemies is "simply the greatest challenge on earth," author R.T. Kendal writes:

> "Jesus uses the word *agape*, as Paul would use in 1 Corinthians 13. It is not *eros* (physical or sexual love), nor *philia* (brotherly love). *Agape* is selfless concern. It is self-giving love. It is not necessarily affection. You may love a person and not want to spend a holiday with them. You may love a person and not like them; but you can act unselfishly."[154]

Commenting on the command to "overcome evil with good" Ken Sande summarises succinctly, "Here then is the ultimate weapon: *deliberate focused love* (Luke 6:27-28; 1 Corinthians 13:4-7). Sometimes this will require going to them to show them their faults. At other times, there may be a need for mercy and compassion, patience, and works of encouragement.

---

[154]R.T. Kendall, *Total Forgiveness* (Hodder & Stoughton Ltd, London, 2010), 157.

Perhaps one of the best examples I could cite is found in 2 Kings chapter 5. The events take place during a period of conflict between the Israelites and their Syrian neighbours. The heroine of the story, who does not even get a name, is a young servant girl who has been taken captive by the Syrian army and is now a slave to the wife of a prominent military commander called Naaman. Although a man of mighty standing, Naaman is found to be struck down with leprosy. Upon seeing the plight of her master, the young servant girl approaches her mistress, Naaman's wife, and recites the one line attributed to her in the entire story when she says: *"If only my master were with the prophet who is in Samaria! For he would heal him of his leprosy"* (2 Kings 5:3). As the story unfolds, Naaman makes his way to Israel, where he eventually seeks out the prophet Elisha, who subsequently gives Naaman a set of instructions, which, when followed, cure him of his leprosy. However, not only is Naaman cured of the disease, but the experience also brings him to faith in the one true God and causes him to declare: *"Indeed, now I know that there is no God in all the earth, except in Israel"* (v 15).

The moral of the story is simply this. The young servant girl who had been forcibly abducted from her family and homeland, had every reason to despise Naaman and everything he represented. She had every reason to refuse to interact with those around her. Yet this little girl, in a display of faith, still had the best interests of her master at heart. She felt compassion for her master's plight as he slowly succumbed to the incurable disease of leprosy. The climax of the story, however, comes when, as a result of that genuine witness of faith, Naaman himself joins the young servant girl in that faith in the one true God.

I would suggest, therefore, that this benevolent love and basic concern for one's fellow man, regardless of the circumstances, is what Jesus meant by the command to *"love your enemies, bless those who curse you, do good to those who hate you"* (Matthew 5:44a) and also what Paul has in mind when he stated, *"If your enemy is hungry, feed him; If he is thirsty, give him a drink"* (Romans 12:20). Such actions have the very real potential to "heap coals of fire" on someone's head, which literally means to cause them to feel remorse by returning good for evil. While the motivation for displaying such genuine concern should never be self-gain, it is worth noting that God promises great reward for those who do so (Proverbs 25:21-22).

Summarising therefore, in practical terms what it might entail to implement Jesus' command to, *"Love your neighbour as yourself"* (Matthew 22:39) and *"Do unto others as you would have them do unto you"* (Matthew 7:12), David Augsburger writes: "Putting this law of reciprocity into personal relationships means at least the following:

○ We listen to others as we want to be listened to.

○ We offer help to others where we would like to be helped.

○ We care more about dealing fairly with our neighbour than we worry about being cheated by our neighbour.

○ We offer praise and appreciation to others as we would want to be appreciated.

○ We treat employees, creditors, and debtors as we would wish to be treated by those in authority over us.

○ We pass on no gossip about another that we would not want circulated about ourselves.

○ We discard all prejudices that we would resent as unfair if we were members of the race or group suffering discrimination.

○ We respect, defend, and accept a person of any race, culture, or class as we would wish to be regarded by them.[155]

Vengeance is Mine

Returning for one last time to Romans 12:17-21, and to what I contend is the most significant phrase of all, *"Vengeance is Mine, I will*

---

[155]David Augsburger, The New Freedom of Forgiveness, 135-136.

repay, says the Lord" (v 19). As we continue to expose the false premise that failure to forgive an unrepentant offender inevitably leads to feelings of resentment and hatred, we now examine one of the great truths of the Christian faith; a truth which may be a comfort to some, but equally which must serve as a very real warning to others. The liberal Christian worldview, where unconditional forgiveness is taken for granted, is, by and large, the same Christian worldview in which God's love is elevated at the expense of all other attributes. The truth that God is also a God of justice, and even, dare I suggest, a vengeful God, is seldom acknowledged today, with the result that the biblical teaching on forgiveness becomes skewed. In this environment, it is not surprising that those who would harbour thoughts of, or worse still, actively pursue revenge, have concluded that God is not capable of doing the job Himself.

However, in again cautioning against such acts of revenge, the apostle Paul writes here in Romans 12:19: *"Beloved, do not avenge yourselves, but rather give place to wrath; for it is written, Vengeance is Mine, I will repay, says the Lord."* It is vitally important, therefore, to keep a balanced view of God in mind, and recognise that He is still a God of justice. Addressing this very point, theologian John Piper writes: "What I find in the New Testament is that one powerful way of overcoming bitterness and revenge is to have faith in the promise that God will settle accounts with our offenders so that we don't have to."[156]

Coincidently, the apostle Paul also presents us with an example of this teaching in relation to an encounter with Alexander the coppersmith. When writing to Timothy, Paul issues this word of caution: *"Alexander the coppersmith did me much harm. May the Lord repay him according to his works. You also must beware of him, for he has greatly resisted our words"* (2 Timothy 4:14-15). Here we see Paul warning Timothy to be aware of Alexander, but most significantly, we also see how Paul himself has resolved to deal with Alexander. While we are not privy as to whether any attempt at reconciliation had taken place between Paul and Alexander, and even if such a discussion had taken place, clearly

---

[156]John Piper, *Future Grace,* (Multnomah Publishers, Sisters, Oregon, USA, 1995), 261.

it would appear to have ended without forgiveness or reconciliation in accordance with Jesus' teaching in Matthew 18:15-17. In any case, Paul reveals his present attitude towards Alexander when he declares: *"May the Lord repay him according to his works."* Clearly, therefore, Paul had simply left the matter in the hands of a just God.

The clear biblical teaching that an unchangeable God will not let the evil doer go unpunished, and His promise to administer justice (Proverbs 11:21; Isaiah 3:11; Ezekiel 7:9), should cause us to ponder carefully the following. First of all, it is evident that we live in a fallen, sin-stained world. A world in which there will be times when justice is not administered and the evildoer seems to have escaped punishment. Secondly, God promises that although there are those deserving of such punishment who may escape justice in this world, it is certain that one day they will have to give an answer for their actions when they stand before Him on the day of judgement. Sadly, again, due to liberal teaching from a theological perspective, coupled with the growing rejection of any notion of a higher authority in general, an impending "day of Judgement" holds little, or no threat for sinful men. The believer, on the other hand, can take comfort in the knowledge that God is in charge at all times and that justice will ultimately be administered.

Finally, from Romans 12:19 we note the phrase, "I *will* repay." Here we see that throughout human history and beyond, God is sovereign, not only over the righteous, but also over the wicked. This is why God can declare in Psalm 2:1-6:

> *"Why do the nations rage, and the people plot a vain thing? The kings of the earth set themselves, and the rulers take counsel together, against the Lord and against His Anointed, saying, "Let us break Their bonds in pieces and cast away Their cords from us." He who sits in the heavens shall laugh; The Lord shall hold them in derision. Then He shall speak to them in His wrath, and distress them in His deep displeasure: "Yet I have set My King On My holy hill of Zion."*

It is imperative, therefore, that we display a humble reverence concerning the judgement of God. Anything less will have us gloating over the perceived destiny of others, when the Christian response should be to show compassion for those who are far removed from the reality of their ultimate destiny. Jay Adams writes of the conflicting obligations placed on those who have suffered a grievous wrong: "You are not obliged to forgive an unrepentant sinner, but you are obliged to try to bring him to repentance."[157]

---

[157]Jay E. Adams, *From Forgiven to Forgiving* (Calvary Press, Amityville, NY, 1994), 36.

Chapter Sixteen

All Things Work for Good

As pointed out at the commencement of this study, the truths contained in Romans 8:28 have become the bedrock of my faith, and indirectly, have even formed the foundation for this study. Turning again, therefore, to the Apostle Paul's letter to the believers in Rome, we read: *"And we know that all things work together for good to those who love God, to those who are the called according to His purpose."* Without doubt, one of the most difficult concepts for us to come to terms with is the reference in this passage to "all things." The thought that God is not only in control of *all things*, but is also directing *all things* towards His eternal purpose, is simply beyond the comprehension of the finite mind.

I am often bemused, for example, by sects like the Jehovah Witnesses, who go to great pains to deny the Christian doctrine of the trinity and, by implication, claim to be able to determine the very nature and makeup of God, the eternal deity who created the vastness of the universe. In response, I am tempted to ask the question: Who do we really think we are, when we confidently assert that we have reached a definitive conclusion on such matters? Relying rather on the Word of God alone, we note that there are limitations to our human understanding of God, and it is perfectly feasible therefore to conclude with Job when he declares: "As *touching the Almighty, we cannot find him out*" (Job 37:23). (KJV)

Recognising our human frailty when it comes to understanding God and the outworking of His divine plans, the apostle Paul also concludes: *"Oh, the depth of the riches both of the wisdom and knowledge of God! How unsearchable are His judgments and His ways past finding out! "For who has known the mind of the Lord? Or who has become His counsellor?"* (Romans 11:33-34). Returning therefore to Romans 8:28, may I suggest that we simply trust the Inspired Word and take the passage at face value, allowing God to reveal those vital truths necessary for our edification and encouragement; the primary lesson in this instance is of course, that God is always in control.

God is Sovereign

As regards the sovereignty of God over "all things," including creation itself (Psalm 135:6-7; Colossians 1:16-17; Revelation 4:11), over governments (Proverbs 21:1; Daniel 2:20-21), over individual lives (John 6:39; Romans 9:15-16; Ephesians 1:11-12), and even over the smallest sparrow which falls from the tree (Matthew 10:29), Ken Sande declares: "God has ultimate control over all that happens in the world." Recognising the enormity of such a proposition, Sande points us to King David, who struggled to understand the wonders of God's intimate involvement in his life, only to conclude: *"Such knowledge is too wonderful for me; It is high, I cannot attain it"* (Psalm 139:6).[158]

Nonetheless, in our attempts to make sense of what goes on around us, the temptation is often to judge God's ways according to our own ideas of what is right or wrong. In stating that, "Such thoughts show how little we understand and respect God," Ken Sande quotes the prophet Isaiah, who warns against such reasoning when he proclaims: "Surely you have things turned around! Shall the potter be esteemed as the clay? For shall the thing made say of him who made it, He did not make me? Or shall the thing formed say of him who formed it, He has no understanding?"[159]

The truth proclaimed, therefore, is that God is indeed sovereign and exercises ultimate control even over painful and unjust events. We

---

[158]Ken Sande, *The Peace Maker*, 60.
[159]Ibid., 61.

see this principle exemplified no more so than in the life story of Joseph (Genesis chapters 37 and 39-50). Having become jealous of Joseph because of his apparent aloofness and their father's favouritism towards their younger sibling, his older brothers seize an opportunity and sell Joseph into slavery in Egypt. Joseph is subsequently sold to Potiphar, a high-ranking Egyptian official, and in time becomes a much-trusted slave in his charge. However, after being falsely accused of impropriety by Potiphar's wife, Joseph is cast into prison for many years. Eventually, Joseph's ability to interpret dreams is brought to Pharaoh's attention, and having successfully predicted an ensuing famine in the land, which in turn allowed for precautionary measures to be implemented, Joseph is elevated to a position of authority over the land of Egypt, answerable only to Pharaoh himself.

With Egypt spared the effects of the famine, occupants of the surrounding countries are forced to travel to Egypt in search of food. And as providence would have it, who should come to Joseph in need of help, only his brothers, who sold him into slavery all those years before. Now, after his time in servitude to Potiphar, not to mention the many years of false imprisonment, some would excuse Joseph for harbouring a festering resentment and thoughts of revenge against his brothers. On the contrary however, Joseph is filled with compassion for these men, and after a short period during which he tests their trustworthiness, Joseph is overcome with emotion as he reveals his identity to his brothers. In relaying the fact that he bears them no animosity, Joseph tells his brothers that throughout all that has taken place, God was ultimately in charge of events. He states:

> *"But now, do not therefore be grieved or angry with yourselves because you sold me here; for God sent me before you to preserve life. For these two years the famine has been in the land, and there are still five years in which there will be neither plowing nor harvesting. And God sent me before you to preserve a posterity for you in the earth, and to save your lives by a great deliverance. So **now it was not you who sent me here, but God**"* (Genesis 45:5-8).

The overarching lesson of the story is the sovereignty of God and the fact that He will always bring about His desired purposes for good. We see Joseph revealing this truth for a second time later in the story, when it became apparent that his brothers were still fearful that he harboured thoughts of revenge. In assuring his brothers again that he held no grudge against them, Joseph reiterates the truth pertaining to the course of events as they had unfolded when he declares: *"You meant evil against me; but God meant it for good"* (Genesis 50:20).

For someone who has suffered a grievous wrong, like so many involved in the conflict in Northern Ireland, particularly when the offence has resulted in the loss of life of a loved one, the providence and sovereignty of God over the affairs of men is an extremely difficult issue to come to terms with. Time and time again, thoughts of missed opportunities, an empty seat at special occasions, are a cruel reminder of what might have been, and it is difficult to see beyond that moment. Yet if God's Word is to bring any comfort in such circumstances, it must be the truth that nothing happens outside of God's control. For those who may still understandably struggle with their particular circumstances, Pastor Chris Brauns seeks to bring encouragement and a sense of perspective, as he shares his take on the implication of Romans 8:28:

> "If you feel yourself wrestling with bitterness, then focus more intently on our glorious God. Savour the providence of God. He is in control of all things. He is perfectly just and cannot be unjust. Bitterness reigns when we have been treated unfairly. But if we believe that God will accomplish justice, and if we are simultaneously confident that God is working all things together for our good, if that is our centre, then we beat the stuffing out of bitterness every time."[160]

In conclusion, therefore, what is often presented as forgiveness, which is little more than a self-serving therapeutic exercise, does little to prepare us for the evil we must face in this world, and particularly the evil that many victims and survivors have had to face in Northern

---

[160]Chris Brauns, *Unpacking Forgiveness* (Crossway, Wheaton, Illinois, 2008), 158.

Ireland. More importantly, however, it undermines the justice of God, and declares that we have a better way of resolving disputes and administering forgiveness, in much the same way that many today pick and choose to elevate those attributes of God that best suit their particular vision of Christianity. Yes, the never-ending love and mercy of God for His children, reflected perfectly in the Cross of Christ, is vitally important; however, majoring on these attributes at the expense of the justice of God undermines the biblical basis for understanding forgiveness.

It can be disheartening when, despite the best efforts of those who have willingly fulfilled their Christian obligation to love their enemies and pray for those who spitefully use them and persecute them, there is still no sign of remorse. Without this elementary basis for forgiveness, the matter then rests entirely in the hands of a Holy God, who will administer justice. It was this great truth that was espoused by Gordon Wilson. Having sincerely prayed for those who had murdered his daughter Marie, Gordon was still acutely aware that, despite his best efforts, it was ultimately up to God Himself to forgive, and to quote Gordon's words again, "on God's terms."

Chapter Seventeen

Be Reconciled

As stated throughout this study, an act of forgiveness which does not result in some kind of reconciled relationship between the parties involved, is not forgiveness as God intended. This, therefore, is where all propositions which involve unconditional "inner" forgiveness, or indeed, the unconditional "offering" of forgiveness, fall short. By way of covering this shortfall, therefore, again as has been pointed out, those who would promote unconditional forgiveness, seek to separate forgiveness entirely from reconciliation. For example, theologian and author Wendy Alsup writes: "Not every relationship will reach reconciliation. It is possible to forgive those who do not see their need to be forgiven... But full reconciliation requires more." Continuing to distinguish the difference between forgiveness and reconciliation, Alsup continues, "The work of *reconciliation is a two-way street.*"[161]

On the contrary, if we are genuine about forgiving as God forgives, then again we must note that the divine model of forgiveness, which itself involves *both parties*, always leads to reconciliation (2 Corinthians 5:18-20). As reconciliation is therefore the natural follow-on goal, it is perhaps necessary to ascertain what a reconciled relationship might look like. To this end, Ken Sande provides a practical synopsis:

> "Being reconciled does not mean that the person who offended you must now become your closest friend. What it means is that your relationship will be at least

[161]Wendy Alsup, I Forgive You (The Good Book Company, 2022), 94.

as good as it was before the offence occurred. Once that happens, an even better relationship may develop."[162]

That said, however, it must also be recognised that in cases where the divisions and disputes find their origins in long-established communal divisions, as in the case of Northern Ireland, reconciliation between individuals may take longer to mature due to the surrounding influences from wider society. Nonetheless, even reconciliation between communities must start somewhere, and as individuals who have experienced the worst of the atrocities become reconciled and develop a growing respect and appreciation for each other, there is every hope that such a spirit of reconciliation will in time challenge others.

Speaking into such a position, by way of specifically addressing what he refers to as "intense and prolonged conflict," Ken Sande also acknowledges the complexities involved. In quoting the saying, "If you are coasting, you must be going downhill," Sande stresses that in these circumstances, "unless a deliberate effort is made to restore and strengthen a relationship, it will generally deteriorate."[163] By way therefore of enabling an offended party to overcome the problems which may arise, Sande proposes three levels on which to peruse reconciliation: in *thought*, *word*, and *deed*.

In relation to "thought," Sande warns, there is a tendency to dwell on "what others have done to hurt us. Try as we might, memories of the offence keep popping back into our minds, and we find ourselves reliving all kinds of painful feelings."[164] In order to counter such thoughts, Sande recommends what he terms the "replacement principle," where one might replace negative thoughts and memories with positive ones, and references Philippians 4:8 by way of encouragement:

> *"Finally, brethren, whatever things are true, whatever things are noble, whatever things are just, whatever things are pure, whatever things are lovely, whatever things are of good report, if there is any virtue and if there is anything praiseworthy-- meditate on these things."*

[162]Ken Sande, The Peace Maker, 219.
[163]Ibid., 219.
[164]Ibid., 220.

Where an offence has been "covered in love" and forgiveness applied (Matthew 5:25), or where an offender has been brought to a position of repentance, and similarly forgiveness has been granted (Luke 17:3), there will always be positives to be drawn from such situations. Considering how your experiences may be of benefit to future generations, particularly within your own family, as you offer advice and counsel, may help when trying to focus on a positive perspective. Such thoughts, I would suggest, are indeed *praiseworthy*.

When we think upon our "words," we are reminded again of James 3:5-8, where the apostle declares that though the *"tongue" is small, it "kindles" a great "fire… no man can tame the tongue. It is an unruly evil, full of deadly poison."* When speaking about someone who may have wronged us in the past, it often takes a conscious effort to be more positive than negative. Again, care should be taken to emphasise the positive outcomes as a result of a reconciled relationship, and in so doing, you will not only encourage the offender but also those around you.

When in harmony, positive thoughts and words will inevitably manifest themselves in "deeds." As C.S. Lewis reputedly said, "Don't waste your time bothering whether you 'love' your neighbour; act as if you did." To which Ken Sande adds, "When you are behaving as if you loved someone, you will presently come to love him.[165] While it is much easier to envisage the effects that positive actions might have in a relationship where there is some degree of regular interaction, it is more difficult to imagine a type of positive action one could direct towards someone with whom you have little or no contact. Where the offence against you was initially committed by someone you didn't know, a positive attitude towards the repentant offender can always be maintained, for example, through prayer. It is often in the place of prayer that we will experience the grace of God, which enables us to remain positive, and as I will seek to explain, prayer itself can become the believer's secret weapon when dealing with conflict.

---

[165]Ibid., 221.

Praying For Our Enemies

While R.T. Kendall, as previously stated, proposes that the command to love one's enemies is "the greatest challenge on earth," I would venture to suggest that Jesus' accompanying command in Matthew 5:44b, to *"pray for those who spitefully use you and persecute you,"* must rank a very close second. With a view, therefore, to grasping the significance of praying for those who persecute you, and in light of the previous point as regards displaying a benevolent love and basic concern for others, the question I would ask is this: within the Christian realm, what is the best we could desire for another? Suffice to say, we are not envisaging that they might win the lottery, whereupon all their earthly desires might be fulfilled, not least because such a material blessing will do little or nothing to alter the heart. Rather, it must be the desire of the believer that all men be brought to a position of repentance and faith in the Lord Jesus Christ. Only such a transformation has the power to bring men to a recognition of past wrongs committed, and convict them of their sin, not only against their fellow man, but more importantly, against a Holy God. And indeed, we remind ourselves that that was the very purpose of Jesus' prayer on the cross and also the apostle Stephen's dying petition. And again, when we reflect on the miraculous answer to those prayers that we looked at earlier, the challenge is, can we begin to imagine the ramifications today if even the most "vilest offender" (to quote the hymn writer) was to be brought to a position of repentance and faith?

There is, however, one major misconception that hinders many from being able to contemplate praying for an offender, and it is found, amongst other places, in the words of the aforementioned hymn, "To God be the Glory," written by Fanny Crosby. The line which references the "offender" reads: "The vilest offender who truly believes, that moment from Jesus a pardon receives." Again, many lose sight of the wider implications of an offender repenting of past wrongs and focus rather on the misconception that such an offender could be *pardoned*, and in effect, let off scot-free.

To take a step back first of all, it is true that when someone comes to "believe on the Lord Jesus Christ," they are justified before God and "saved" (Acts 16:31); their transgressions are removed *"as far as the east is from the west"* (Psalm 103:12) and there remains *"no condemnation to those who are in Christ Jesus"* (Romans 8:1). However, the Bible does not teach that those who have been forgiven by God will not have to face the consequences of their past sin. Rather, for the remainder of their lives, to one degree or another, they will have to live with those consequences.

Ken Sande agrees when he writes, "Forgiveness does not automatically release a wrongdoer from all the consequences of sin. Although God forgave the Israelites who rebelled against him in the wilderness, He decreed that they would die without entering the Promised Land (Numbers 14:20-23).[166] The life of Israel's King David also bears perfect testimony to this truth. Having arranged for Uriah to be strategically placed in battle in order that he be killed, with the sole intention of taking Uriah's wife Bathsheba as his own, King David is later confronted with his sin by Nathan the prophet (2 Samuel 12:1-7). In pronouncing judgement upon David, Nathan declares:

> *"Thus says the Lord God of Israel: 'I anointed you king over Israel, and I delivered you from the hand of Saul. I gave you your master's house and your master's wives into your keeping, and gave you the house of Israel and Judah. And if that had been too little, I also would have given you much more! Why have you despised the commandment of the Lord, to do evil in His sight? You have killed Uriah the Hittite with the sword; you have taken his wife to be your wife, and have killed him with the sword of the people of Ammon. Now therefore, the sword shall never depart from your house, because you have despised Me, and have taken the wife of Uriah the Hittite to be your wife.' Thus says the Lord: 'Behold, I will raise up adversity against you from your own house; and I will take your wives before your eyes and give them to your neighbour,*

---

[166]Ken Sande, *The Peace Maker*, 212.

*and he shall lie with your wives in the sight of this sun. For you
did it secretly, but I will do this thing before all Israel, before
the sun"* (2 Samuel 12:7-12).

While David's immediate response was confession, and sincere
repentance (see Psalm 51), the Lord did not withdraw His Holy
discipline. As a consequence, David was to bear the consequences
of his sin for the remainder of his life. First, the child that David
had with Bathsheba died. This tragic event was followed up with
strife within David's family; one of his sons, Amnon, raped David's
daughter Tamar; another son, Absalom, subsequently killed Amnon,
before later attempting to actually overthrow King David himself.
So, when we enter into prayer on behalf of an offender, earnestly
seeking for them to come to repentance and faith in Jesus Christ, let
us humbly bear in mind that, in this life, they will never really be free
of the *consequences* of their previous actions, which may even include
having to answer to a court of law for crimes committed.

Chapter Eighteen

In Conclusion

The primary purpose for undertaking this study was to address what I referred to in the introduction as, the "disconnect" between victims and survivors who still bear the physical and psychological scars of the conflict, and the only source of divine healing able to bring comfort in such circumstances. The prevailing theological view that biblical forgiveness must be unconditionally granted in every circumstance, regardless of the seriousness of the crime, has retraumatised many victims and survivors. For various reasons, they find that they are unable to come to such a position. Albeit, perhaps inadvertently therefore, this teaching of unconditional forgiveness has thrown many victims and survivors, particularly those from within the faith community, into a state of confusion, with many more simply walking away from their faith altogether, unable to come to terms with the perceived injustice of such teaching.

With specific reference to post-conflict Northern Ireland, however, many well-intentioned church leaders and representatives will proclaim that the enactment of unconditional forgiveness is the only way to achieve lasting peace. The pursuit of peace, therefore, or, dare I suggest a 'worldly' definition of peace, is presented as the ultimate goal, even if the pursuit of this so-called peace necessitates compromising biblical principles.

The first principle in relation to biblical forgiveness which falls foul of this compromising approach, is the command to "rebuke" or "tell a brother his fault," with a view to bringing the offender to a position of repentance (Luke 17:3; Matthew 18:15-17). The truth of Scripture declares that where offences are so serious as to undermine the stability of family, community, or wider society, then it is imperative that the offender be confronted. While again, many well-meaning church representatives will be quick to point out that they have always called for justice to be administered in relation to the many crimes committed during the conflict, the fact remains that when it comes to calling on the perpetrators to *repent*, the voices tend to die down, or worse still, by promoting unconditional forgiveness, the blame is shifted to the victims and survivors by inferring that it is a sin not to forgive the unrepentant terrorist who has caused them so much pain. Those who follow such a path would do well to heed Proverbs 24:24-25 which declares, *"He who says to the wicked, "You are righteous," Him the people will curse; Nations will abhor him. But **those who rebuke the wicked will have delight,** and a good blessing will come upon them."*

Again, it is difficult not to conclude that many shy away from the task of rebuking offenders and calling out their faults, declaring once more that such a stance might cause offence and adversely affect that quest for peace. On the contrary, when Jesus found it necessary to confront His enemies, He did not hold back from giving those who opposed Him their *historical and cultural pedigree*. Denouncing the "Scribes and Pharisees," Jesus declared to them:

> *"Outwardly [you] appear righteous to men, but inside you are full of hypocrisy and lawlessness… you are sons of those who murdered the prophets. Fill up, then, the measure of your fathers' guilt. Serpents, brood of vipers! How can you escape the condemnation of hell? Therefore, indeed, I send you prophets, wise men, and scribes: some of them you will kill and crucify, and some of them you will scourge in your synagogues and persecute from city to city, that on you may come all the righteous blood shed on the earth, from the blood of righteous Abel to the blood of Zechariah, son of Berechiah, whom you murdered between the temple and the altar"* (Matthew 23:28-35).

The second biblical principle that falls foul of this compromising approach is the fact that Jesus never presents peace in this world as an ultimate goal for the believer. On the contrary, Jesus declares in Luke 12:51 that He did *not* come *"to give peace on earth... but rather division."* And in Mark 13:9-13, Jesus tells his followers that they *"will be beaten in the synagogues," "brought before rulers and kings," "brother would betray brother to death,"* and they *"will be hated by all for my name's sake."*

That is not to deny, of course, that throughout his ministry, Jesus' message was one of peacemaking, and indeed, centuries before he was born, the prophet Isaiah gave our Lord the title, "Prince of Peace" (Isaiah 9:6). However, it must be borne in mind that the peace of which Jesus spoke was to be found in a higher realm. This truth is clearly laid before us in John 14:27, where Jesus declares: *"Peace I leave with you, My peace I give to you;* ***not*** *as the world gives do I give to you."* And the goal of this peace is further defined in Paul's letter to the believers in Ephesus when he writes: *"And He [Jesus] came and preached peace to you who were afar off and to those who were near... Now, therefore, you are no longer strangers and foreigners, but fellow citizens with the saints and members of the household of God"* (Ephesians 2:17-19).

The peace to which Jesus refers is that *"peace of God, which surpasses all human understanding"* (Philippians 4:7) and which brings eternal security and comfort to the soul. This true peace, therefore, is the real ultimate goal for the believer, as confirmed in the words of the Prophet Isaiah when he declares that only those who *"keep the truth may enter in"* and until that day, God *"will keep him in perfect peace, whose mind is stayed on [Him]"* (Isaiah 26:2-3). The peace which Jesus proclaimed, and the peace which He sought to establish therefore, was peace between man and God.

While Christians should *"if possible... live peaceably with all men"* (Romans 12:18), it is nonetheless evident that peace per se, is not the ultimate goal for the believer, not least because there may be occasions when, short of unacceptable compromise, such peace will be beyond reach. The elusiveness of the *world's* peace is painfully evident in the fact that many of those "saints" who refused to compromise, and who were subsequently *"slain for the word of God and for the testimony which they held",* did not receive justice in this life, and still to this day, cry aloud saying, *"How long, O Lord, holy and true, until You judge and avenge our blood on those who dwell on the earth?"* (Revelation 6:9-10)

The final and most important principle that gets undermined by compromising on the biblical teaching of forgiveness is the *justice of God.* All too often, it is man's (and women's) sensitivities that have governed the teaching on repentance and forgiveness. This invariably leads to further error. By way of downplaying the emphasis on repentance, how often have we heard the phrase, "God loves you the way you are"? Well, I'm sorry to say that the truth of Scripture declares that God does *not* love you the way you are; rather God loves his people *in spite* of the way they are. The reality is that prior to conversion, I, like all believers, were so bad that God had to send His son Jesus Christ to die for me, and in so doing, settle the sin debt that was due.

This is the real measure of God's mercy and love, just as the apostle Paul declares in Romans 5:8; *"But God demonstrates His own love toward us, in that **while we were still sinners**, Christ died for us."* By the grace of God, therefore, the believer is brought to a position of repentance and faith, and it is only after this *change*, or *conversion*, that they are welcomed into the family of God. The liberal view of unconditional forgiveness, therefore, leaves a void in the God-ordained justice system, with the result that many today see little merit in what they have been led to believe is biblical forgiveness. The comfort we have in the knowledge that God will one day administer His justice "on His terms" is lost to many, who continue to suffer as a consequence of the many injustices in the world today.

Regrettably, however, forgiveness which leads ultimately to reconciliation, is not always achievable in the real world in which we live, and no amount of perverting God's Word or self-deception will alter that uncomfortable fact. Sadly, the muddying of the waters around the subject of forgiveness and reconciliation, has blinded many to the simple truth which Jesus taught us. In layman's terms, the framework for forgiveness is not that dissimilar to our present-day legal system, in that the more severe the offence, the more severe the measures must be to achieve justice. While minor infringements require little more than a cautionary word, more serious offences will require a police investigation and potentially court action. Likewise with forgiveness, while "love" covers a multitude of minor offences, those more serious offences require that dialogue take place in order, if possible, to achieve repentance, forgiveness, and reconciliation. The one major difference, however, is that while evil men may lie with a view to escaping justice in our court system, no amount of fabricated evidence, either on the part of the offender or his paid legal representatives, will enable him to escape the justice of God. In Psalm 37:1-15, King David is able to declare therefore:

> *"Do not fret because of evildoers, Nor be envious of the workers of iniquity. For they shall soon be cut down like the grass, And wither as the green herb…. For evildoers shall be cut off; But those who wait on the Lord, They shall inherit the earth. For yet a little while and the wicked shall be no more; Indeed, you will look carefully for his place, But it shall be no more…. The wicked plots against the just, And gnashes at him with his teeth. The Lord laughs at him, For He sees that his day is coming. The wicked have drawn the sword And have bent their bow, To cast down the poor and needy, To slay those who are of upright conduct. Their sword shall enter their own heart, and their bows shall be broken."*

While the fate of the wicked is spelled out clearly here, it must also be recognised that within the above passage, the Psalmist also exhorts those who have suffered at the hands of such wicked men when he writes:

> *"Trust in the Lord, and do good; Dwell in the land, and feed on His faithfulness…. Rest in the Lord, and wait patiently for Him; Do not fret because of him who prospers in his way, Because of the man who brings wicked schemes to pass. Cease from anger, and forsake wrath; Do not fret – it only causes harm."*

There is no doubt that wicked men have caused great harm and, in many instances, continue to do so. However, such actions on the part of these men do not negate the command to "Trust in the Lord" and to "do good." As has already been highlighted, "doing good" involves having the grace to forgive unconditionally, even the most heinous of crimes, when the circumstances, by way of repentance, have been met. But just as importantly, doing good also involves, with the help of God's grace, seeking to develop an attitude of willingness to forgive, in the genuine hope that past wrongs committed on the part of an offender will be renounced and genuine repentance forthcoming. With the way now open for reconciliation to be achieved, we can truly "forsake wrath" and "dwell in the land, and feed on [God's] faithfulness."

While such a concept still seems difficult to many, Bishop Desmond Tutu presents this challenging question when he asks, "Aren't some people just evil, just monsters, and aren't such people just unforgivable?" In replying to his own question, he writes:

> "I do believe there are monstrous and evil acts but I do not believe those who commit such acts are monsters or evil. To relegate someone to the level of monster is to deny that person's ability to change and to take away that person's accountability for his or her actions and behaviour."[167]

Bishop Tutu concludes, "Let us condemn ghastly acts, but let us never relinquish the hope that the doers of the most heinous deeds can and may change."[168]

At the beginning of this study, I posed the following question to myself and to the victims and survivors of terrorist violence: "Can we truly adhere to the words of Jesus as recorded in Matthew 5:44-45, when He calls on believers to, *"love your enemies, bless those who curse you, do good to those who hate you, and pray for those who spitefully use you and persecute you."* In closing, it is my prayerful desire that, in light of a correct understanding of biblical forgiveness, many will

---

[167]Desmond & Mpho Tutu, *The Book Of Forgiving* (William Collins, London, 2015), 55.
[168]Ibid., 57.

find it easier to not only see the perpetrators in a different light, but that many will be able to read our Lord's challenging words here in Matthew chapter 5 and truly ponder the immense ramifications they entail for everyone.

When discussing the fledgling Northern Ireland peace process with my late father back in 1998, he stated: "If we are ever to have a lasting peace, one side will have to wipe the other side out; either that or we must learn to live together." He was, of course, highlighting the impossibility, not to mention the senseless barbarity of the former solution by way of advocating the latter. Not surprisingly, when it comes to living together and avoiding conflict, Jesus provides us with what Ken Sande calls the "Golden Rule," as recorded in Matthew 7:12: *"Therefore, whatever you want men to do to you, do also to them, for this is the Law and the Prophets."*[169]

---

[169]Ken Sande, *The Peace Maker*, 124.

TO CONTACT THE AUTHOR EMAIL

standingonthepromises1998@gmail.com

INSPIRED TO WRITE A BOOK?

Contact

Maurice Wylie Media

Your Inspirational & Christian Book Publisher

Based in Northern Ireland and distributing around the world.

www.MauriceWylieMedia.com